QUIET SITTING

QUIET SITTING

The Daoist Approach
for a Healthy Mind and Body

By Chen Yingning & Jiang Weiqiao
With an Introduction by Yanling Johnson

Better Link Press

Taoism was the earliest philosophy, anywhere in the Oikoumenê, to surmise that Man, in achieving civilization, might have compromised his position in the Universe by putting himself out of harmony with the spirit of the ultimate reality in which Man lives and moves and has his being.

—*Arnold Toynbee*

CONTENTS

INTRODUCTION

This translation of the great Daoist Chen Yingning is long overdue! It is a great honor for me to write an introduction for this Daoist guru and I hope more of his many valuable writings will be introduced to the West in the near future.

A reference to the Daoist Immortal School of the present, Chen had no alternative but to do an excerpt on only one part of the "Immortality" lineage as a science project, hoping to get society's attention. The School of Immortality was originated by the Yellow Emperor more than 5,000 years ago, and has branched out into several lineages according to Chen's book. Unfortunately the Immortality School and its lineages have become on the verge of being wiped out during the recent century, when western influences took over much of the traditional culture.

Chinese ancestors believe that humans, nature and the universe share an energy, which they call qi. Along with some Daoists, the Chinese scientists and researchers in the 1980s and 1990s had tried to discover the mystery of qi. And in the process, many of them became qigong practitioners and a few even became enlightened.

Qi Is the Best Energy Resource on Earth

Qi is a Daoist term which refers to the energy that human and nature share. In Chinese culture, it is not only considered the best source of energy, but also the life source to all living things on Earth. Daoism is not a religion. When Buddhism was adopted into the Chinese culture the people were motivated to establish their own native religion, Daoist religion, to coexist harmoniously with it.

The Daoist concept and the practice of qi played, as it still does, a significant role in the Chinese culture, giving it an arsenal of effective tools such as Traditional Chinese Medicine (TCM), healthy eating and living harmoniously with nature. All the tools are used to connect qi with the mind, body and nature. The essential purpose of these tools, called cultivations, is about how to follow the Natural Law. The Chinese have produced various self-help cultivations based on this philosophy. Aside from spiritual pursuit, these tools teach one how to work on habitual patterns, discipline the mind, and refine the qi one has in order to preserve health.

The Existence of Qi

Qi exists. The word and concept of qi seems unfamiliar to the rest of the world although it is commonly used in Chinese culture and in Asian countries. Qi 氣 is written as *ki* in Asian cultures. In Chinese language the original character of qi is 炁. Later on, 炁 was replaced by another character 氣. The concept of the character 炁 refers to the true prenatal energy that a living person is born with and that is so clear it looks as if it is empty.

The knowledge of the existence of qi and how to use it have been well documented in all the ancient Chinese medical and qi practice books. These books were written by experts of Daoism, whom the Chinese refer to as *zhen ren* (true person).

Qi can never be used up because it is infinite and exists throughout the universe. The *Zhuangzi* (or *Nanhua Zhenjing*, *Real Sutra of South China*, written by Zhuangzi, a sage who was closed to Laozi, and later scholars) says, "The whole world and the cosmos are nothing but qi—that's all." And Confucius taught that: "The world is not what we try to explore. The world should be what we learn how to merge and exchange with it, so that we can benefit each other and enhance our power and life."

Because qi has been an essential part of Chinese culture for thousands of years, ordinary Chinese, those with and without schooling, can apply the use of qi to their daily lives. Qi is not elusive to anyone. In fact, we all experience qi. For example, when we relax completely, we feel good; this is because qi flows easily when there is less constriction, less tension. Many people cross their hands subconsciously to retain calm. This is a posture in qigong that helps to center the self with its qi. When one brings both hands together in front of the chest to a praying position, it aims at one of our energy centers—the middle Dantian (below the heart), which is related to the heart. As a result, this posture can guide qi to the middle Dantian and the person becomes calm down and gathered. By using these simple postures, qi energy can recharge us.

Qi and *Xin*: "Two in One"

In the Chinese language, the English concept of both heart and mind has only one word, *xin*. The *xin* word is widely used in the Chinese language, culture, custom, daily life, health care and traditional medicine. *Xin* is a very special part of the human being. It is different from all the rest of the organs, including the brain. This is why it is the only Chinese character written differently from the hard and soft organs and the rest of the body parts. All the body parts include a flesh-part called the moon (月 meaning flesh), except the *xin* character. (In this moon meaning flesh concept hides yet another Daoist life "secret" because Daoism thinks the moon energy affects human vital energy.) The way *xin* 心 is written hints that *xin* is not of flesh or material. The organ of *xin*, the heart, is not the true *xin* but considered its "borrowed house." "Secrets" about the human life like these are indicated in many Chinese traditional characters, and in terms, idioms, and even sayings created by the Chinese ancestors.

Going beyond the understanding of Western medicine and science, and of common understanding, both Daoism and the religion of Buddhism believe that *xin* is a pure, quiet, and very fine energy that is imageless, shapeless, and looks empty. The origin of the *xin* is ever changing no matter the condition, situation, and time. How to transform the human *xin* by instruction and cultivation back to its purity or void (also called the "origin") is the aim of Daoism and Buddhism as well.

To explain *xin* in western terms, when this quiet original qi begins moving, the movement is called the mind; and when it becomes still and quiet, it is the true heart. So the heart and the mind are two sides of one origin, one still and one moving. This means the quiet and true still heart is the true self. As a Buddhist guru described: "When the sand grains in a cup of water sunk, the water becomes clear." He used this example to explain how our mind becomes clear. Also, extra sensory abilities may be revealed and phenomena can occur. This philosophy is well displayed and defined in the bagua chart, the *I Jing* (*Book of Change*), the five elements theory, and the yin yang theories. It is expressed as well in the Buddhist practice "In Emptiness the supernatural exist."

Because of the phenomena, self *xin* is hard for ordinary people to understand and difficult to explore, which prompted the Yellow Emperor's warning to not teach superstitious people the qigong (called *daoyin* 导引, mind guides the qi, then). This is because wisdom needs to be cultivated alongside extra sensory abilities in more advanced practice. Buddhism also teaches "Wisdom is the mother of a Buddha."

This is the reason why the Chinese ancient teachings put emphasis on the cultivation of self *xin*. Such self-cultivation has developed into various approaches and formed a culture. For example, a polite Chinese way to mention to "bathe" is *muyu* 沐浴. Both the characters have a water-drops on the left side; the word 沐 includes woods 木 and the other 浴 includes valley 谷. The term to bathe indicates that to bathe means cleansing qi in nature. We do feel more relaxed and cleansed in the woods, don't we? So to bathe in nature brings the practitioner is closer to the true self as we become more carefree. As you can see now how Daoism is used as a way of cultivated living. Even the Daoist temple name indicates this. A Daoist temple is not called temple or monastery, but *guan* 观, which means "to observe and learn, to behold."

To self-cultivate the *xin* through learning with wisdom is a shared principle by all the lineages of qigong. So this is the main principle in Buddhism and Confucianism, except they teach and practice in their own characteristic ways. The lineages are created by those enlightened gurus, adepts, and those who have become the Buddhas and immortals. The various lineages are created because of these masters' different paths to enlightenment. Because of its origin, the Daoist styles emphasize more on the physical other than *xin* cultivation. Thus its off-springs developed like the different styles of martial arts, taiji (taichi), etc. Buddhism on the other hand focuses more on the *xin* cultivation, as a result it has developed many adaptive ways to cultivate the human *xin*. Yet, at the top of the cultivating path, all is empty; a very, very fine energy that seems like a void that both Daoism and Buddhism agrees with.

The Chinese culture has accumulated profound knowledge of qi and *xin* in its 5,000 years of history, giving it the power to ensure a lasting civilization that withstood its own historical tests. This qi culture is capable of enduring because its vital energy links everything: tradition, language, life style, health care, and spiritual practices. Qi also links to the minority groups and the spring cultures.

All of these originated from Daoism.

Daoism emphasizes both qi and *xin* because *xin* is the qi. The indication of *xin* and qi as "two in one" is found in almost everything in Chinese culture relating to life. Without qi there is no *xin*, so then there won't be intuition; without qi there is no life. Since there is not a language that can exactly describe this perfect, vital qi origin within each living person, Daoism used "-" to refer to it, as in the book of the *I Ching*. In terms of Buddhism, this is called the "Buddha nature." However, this little perfect "-" does not refer to a regular soul that is another stage of qi. To explain this in a more modern sense, we may think that the lineages of qigong, taiji, and Confucianism, as well as Buddhism, all are tools for us to choose from, used to repair the connection of intuition between the brain and *xin* (heart+mind) and the body, and so on.

The truth from my own "digging" is that when you get to the bottom of it all you will find that the shared principles and practices of Daoism and Buddhism is all about how to follow the Natural Law. This is why there has never been a conflict between the two main Chinese religions even though they have differences. Thus, qigong now embraces Buddhist and Daoist styles.

Qigong

Here is the definition of Qigong:

QI = ENERGY

GONG = SKILL

QIGONG = THE SKILL OF ATTRACTING VITAL ENERGY

Qigong is a self-healing art that combines movement
and meditation.

Visualizations are employed to enhance the mind/body
connection and assist healing.

Regular practice of qigong can:

- prevent and treat illness

- reduce stress—establish balance

- integrate mind/body/spirit—bring peace

The term qigong was first used by Immortal Xu Zhi-
yang (279 – 374) (according to the *Qigong Dictionary* published by Renmin Weisheng Publication, China, printed in
1988). Before that the qi practice was called *daoyin*. The
qigong theory is that all living beings' qi energy move, will-
ingly or not, in the same routine and pattern. It is the same
cycle as the Natural Law, which is seasonal and with which

a person should comply. When following the cycle of nature a person can use qi to heal self, prevent diseases, enjoy a lasting healthy life, and can even learn to heal others.

Qigong includes both moving forms and quiet forms. The physical moving types, according to individual needs, are designed for building up and cleansing the body's qi that can "assist" the practitioner to calm the mind. Its function is to remove the stagnation of blood so the blocked qi circulation will flow well. Otherwise, a health problem, including a serious illness like cancer can develop. The qi theory and its practice is a way to open up the qi channels and soothe the mind that are both directly related to true self heart. Although moving forms help heal and promote the qi channels to circulate, the opening up of the entire body can only happen during the quiet, still forms and mostly in sitting posture.

For a beginner, the best way to learn is to focus on one type first because only focusing can help a beginner gain some understanding. Then choose according to one's own interest and preference. Focusing on one lineage is very important. Afterwards he or she can study the various differences between the lineages and decide. All the beginning levels can improve health and heal. However, not everyone can practice the high levels for various reasons. Most important of all, heart and mind cultivation is the most essential.

Quiet Qigong

Quiet qigong is very important because of the nature in the human's true heart. Our true heart, or called the origin of the *xin*, is not judgmental. It is quiet, tolerant, and carefree. This is why the quiet type of practices can help the practitioner become more peaceful, relaxed, and heal. Its function is to center and calm the mind, soothing the qi within, and as a result the practice can improve health and increase wisdom.

There are many lineage-passed quiet practices such as using breathing, hearing, visualizations, and incantations. Quiet qigong is mostly practiced in a sitting posture with legs crossed, but there are also lying and standing types. Quiet qigong has various styles and different stages. In the following, I introduce a breathing type as one example.

The Taiji School originator, Immortal Zhang Sanfeng, passed down a practice called, "Using natural breathing to locate the immortal self." He taught how to adjust the human way of breathing to return to the "fetus breathing way." This is through natural breathing "to locate own true divine self." Briefly, the way to practice is to gently be aware of one's breath until it becomes long, soft and deep. When the practitioner continuously breathes soft, deep and long, focused with no mind disturbances all the time, his or her body will gradually change. This practice has been used by many different schools and some have developed slightly different methods.

According to the traditional Chinese medical theory, this way of breathing is effective because it connects to the whole face where twelve "qi channels" release their energy. The channels, also called meridians, are used in Daoism and TCM. The main qi channels were discovered by the Daoist adepts who developed their powers and were able to scan the human body. The meridians are used to treat diseases and to promote the practitioner's personal cultivation.

The face is connected to the nasal cavity and the brain. When using the natural breathing to locate the true self, all four nasal sinuses and paranasal sinuses are all inhaling and exhaling. This enables the flow of prenatal qi into the brain by connecting to the Du channel (or called the governor meridian, the main channel moving along the spine). As a result, such breathing can stimulate the practitioner's prenatal internal breathing like a fetus.

In qigong theory, the fetus-way breathing (also known as embryonic) is also reconnecting with the invisible born-with qi "pipe" that humans have lost. This qi "pipe" disappears quickly after the baby is born. And the invisible qi "pipe" connects the Qihai (also an acupoint, innner navel) with Shanzhong (middle point between two nipples). When the long, soft breathing way continues, this eventually leads to deep meditation. And when this way of breathing continues the practitioner will shift back to the fetus-breathing way. Then the practitioner is not breathing through the nose but the navel (and also the Baihui point, the spot at the top of your head when your thumbs touch the tops of your ears and your middle fingers reach to, etc.). It is like a baby breathing in the mother's womb. In the book by Daoist Tian Chengyang (a Daoist from the White Cloud Temple who has written a few books and has established a small temple in Spain and now lives there), it says that such accomplished way of breathing through the invisible qi "pipe" connects the prenatal qi in the lower Dantian to Shanzhong.

Some classic books described that when the fetus-like breathing is going to happen the practitioner's nose begins twitching etc. This internal breathing first happens in short bursts.

The experienced practitioners described that the nose is not breathing but the lower abdomen is. In the beginning, this breathing experience is short and will disappear as soon as the mind begins to interrupt. When the practitioner gains more control of letting go of the mind this experience will last longer; and can then experience the skin breathing. It is a cool sensation on the skin when the pores inhale and a warm feeling when the pores exhale. This way of breathing also promotes other potentials to be revealed. Though due to the mind, it is not easy to retain this stable, lasting state. But when the practitioner can retain the state long enough, she or he can enter the ultimate state of feeling of no qi moving at all. All becomes still and tranquil.

The crucial moments are during the more advanced quiet practice when self qi is building up and the mind is increasing power. When the practitioner lacks faith in self, he or she may give up. So to practice long-time quiet meditation one needs a truly good teacher as well as self education.

Qigong Practice Is a Human Science

So many successful masters of the lineages in Chinese history have proven that qi is a divine energy shared by human and all living things with nature and the universe. So qigong is about human life and health. It is ancient, yet a forever young "science." However, only the practitioners can understand this "science." All practitioners have experienced some during self practice. For example, after a good meditation you can feel own forehead skin stretching gently and face relaxed. A long term qi practitioner's skin looks smoother and facial expression looks kind. This practice makes the body and the brain carefree. The result is relaxation, which allows the *xin* to become centered and clear. We often see a kindly face, not weary or tired, on a high-level master. This shows his or her quality of qi. This is the "art work" of qi.

The Chinese culture has given a complete theory and "technology" to help make the best use of the qi resource. There are plenty of facts that qigong practitioners have offered to modern researchers to study this energy. Qi concept has penetrated the Chinese life and become a philosophical guide. Unfortunately even though people live in the qi culture, are using the methods and theory daily in life, many are unaware of this treasure. The qi energy resource has not yet caught most of the world's attention.

To end this section, we may call qigong the oldest "technology" for health care, by working on both the mind and qi energy. No other type of energies or modern technologies created for improving health is as good as the "qi healer within" that heals both the mental and physical. I hope qi health care can promote modern science to scale new heights of human study. However, its profoundness can only be proven by personal experience, not just in laboratories or by studying the theories.

Qi in Language and Philosophy

Anyone who has learned some Chinese language will notice that the qi word is used often. You can discover the qi spirit and terms used by the most regular Chinese who are not informed and those who have little education. It is indicated in their language, their way of thinking, and their life style. For example, when someone says that she or he feels low in energy, the Chinese way of saying is: "The person's qi is weak, deficient." When the Chinese people refer to someone who is well educated, well behaved, intelligent, and honest, they say: "This person's qi quality (qi *zhi*) is good!" To describe a person who is glowing with health and radiating vitality the Chinese way of saying it is: "His or her eyes show the *shen* qi!" To be energetic means this person has plenty of qi. When referring to someone who did a wrong thing, but with good intention, the saying is: "His or her *xin*-qi is good!" The saying for being discouraged or losing hope is: "His qi is draining!" (*xie* qi). The saying for being mad, flustered, and exasperated is: "This person's qi is swift and degenerated (qi *ji bai huai*)."

When the Daoist philosophy is used in politics, it is shown in a leader who brings peace, harmony, and good living conditions to the people. When this philosophy is shown between people, it is kindness, loyalty, and devoted to friendship. This philosophy comes from the word Dao that is commonly translated as the "Way." In the *Dao De Jing*, *De* is commonly defined as "morality." Yet *De* does not simply refer to doing good deeds and being righteous, but more for self-cultivation and refining qi within.

According to Daoism the theory is that qi has no beginning or ending. Thus, qi has always been associated with the universe, or the Big Bang Theory, in which all matter is formed and all creation occurs. This qi energy will turn into wisdom.

Based on this concept, this qi wisdom became the foundation of Chinese philosophy, branched into the Chinese way of health care, which advocates cleansing the qi energy and qi in the organs to balance body and mind. This philosophy is implied in the fluidity of the bagua diagram. This fluidity is well defined in the five elements theory that is called mutual creation and restraint. They are wood, fire, metal, water, and earth all exist within the joined, conjugate qi. And the Daoist theory considers the five elements to represent the five stars: Mars-fire-heart, Saturn-earth-spleen/stomach, Venus-metal-lung, Mercury-water-kidneys, Jupiter-wood-liver. They have direct affect on our earthly lives as they are presented according to the five elements theory used in Chinese medicine. The qi between the five elements promotes each other, affect each other, and also restrain one another as a result of this conjugation. So do the qi movement between these organs. This philosophy is shown in the yin and yang theory; two belonging to one. To use our world to define the yin-yang and life, we may think of our world this way: the atmosphere that protects Earth is protecting a yin-and-yang ball so that lives can be produced and things can grow. Lives are produced and last when the yin and yang energy mingle and merge, following the changing cycles of the five elements. Regular human beings have to live within the protection of the Earth's atmosphere in this yin-and-yang energy-balancing world. When moving beyond the atmosphere, thus getting beyond the yin-and-yang ball, regular human beings lose the protection and cannot survive. As a result, the regular human beings have to stay in the "space ship" that contains oxygen for breathing. However, a person has potential to learn to move beyond the yin-and-yang dimension with no need to stay inside a "space ship." In other words, the human beings who achieved moving beyond the earth yin-yang world, and even beyond the other yin-yang energy dimensions, are called celestials, or Buddhas. This is the essence of the qi philosophy.

Because this balancing yin-yang energy is so humanitarian, qi health care has never been a professionally dominated business even though it has been around for 5,000 years ago. It has developed into a self-education health care philosophy, built by the earliest emperor-sages. The Chinese earliest emperors were great qi master practitioners, experts in eating right, fengshui, and herbal medicine. They built a system that made all the information available to everybody. To achieve balance has become the way in Chinese life and in its traditional medicine. This qi philosophy has been rooted deeply in the people. It has been produced the most well known contributors in Chinese health care history. These people were influential experts, such as Laozi, Zhuangzi, Confucius, Daoism-sage emperors, kings, and officials. This self-help qi care has become an honorable education and quality to the scholars, high officials, and generals. For example, almost all the officials were eager to read *The Compendium of Materia Medica*—a medical work written by Li Shizhen (1518 – 1593) during the Ming Dynasty of China.

In Chinese culture, all great physicians were, and are, all experts on eating right, qi practitioners, and researchers. Some of these experts were, and are, the known Daoists, Confucian scholars, officials, martial arts masters, and Buddhist masters. Many regular people practice and educate themselves with basic herbal medicine knowledge and how to eat right. When a nation is made aware by self-efforts to take care of its own health, as practiced traditionally by the Chinese, and not rely mainly on the professionals, with the government helping to create a supportive environment, this is called true public health care.

Qi Is Human Nature and Human Spirit

A living person is made of qi energy; a soul is qi energy that may be able to cultivate and refine self enlightenment. Such qi cultivation has produced many well-known male and female Immortals who all were experts on eating right, diet, and herbal medicine. These practitioners of Daoism, in their own way, have carried on the way of the Dao. They have been the inspiration in qi care. The terms "*jing* (essence)", "qi," and "*shen* (spirit)" are the terms used to define qi cultivation, and are used commonly in Chinese language.

Daoism believes a living person's body is a tiny "universe," and the body's biological changing must follow the Dao—the natural way of the universe. This is described in the book *I Ching* (*Book of Change*). The essential point of Daoism is to take advantage of the infinite qi energy source in nature and in the universe for good health, longevity, and for spiritual purposes. In this philosophy, self *shen* (spirit)—the true *xin* is the "guardian" that can help repair "qi umbilical cord" that is connected to the universe, metaphorically speaking.

Jing (essence) is the congenital qi that we all are born with. It is lucid and "invisible" to most people's eyes. It is the purest, finest, original qi, and can be seen only by those who reach this level. This energy is cognitive.

The moment when a baby is being born his or her life is primarily made up of qi—the *jing* (essence) springs the yin qi and the yang qi, or called taiji. Base on this theory, this is how the Chinese immortals' cultivate to refine the "springs" until "returning to the origin." However, the *jing*, qi and *shen* that the immortals cultivate according to the classics refer to only the prenatal qi, prenatal *jing*, and prenatal *shen* that all have been cultivated beyond regular body condition. Immortal Qiu Chuji, founder of the Daoist Dragon Gate Lineage, defined it this way:

"Without nourishing the primary qi one cannot gain longevity; without nourishing the primary *shen* one cannot connect with the celestials." All the Daoist classics emphasized that *jing*, qi and *shen* are inseparable from the *xing* 性.

Xing 性 is an essential term used by in both Daoist and Buddhist practices. *Xing* is translated as nature, origin. The following chart may give you some brief idea about how *jing*, qi and *shen* are related to self *xing*—nature.

Shen (awareness, subconscious, the main focus referring to the upper Dantian)

Jing (prenatal essence, in the kidneys; or called Mingmen—the Life gate, a very important point related to the kidneys in lower back. The main focus referring to the lower Dantian)

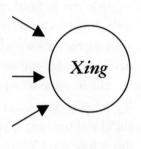

Qi (not objective, but can become an object; never dies out, life source within and from the Cosmos, the main focus referring to the middle Dantian)

From the illustration, you can see that all the three are related to and are from *xing*. So, we may call xing the core, or the fountain of *jing*, qi, and *shen*. When these three merge into one, the practitioner's *xing* will receive plenty of power and begin to reveal the self. According to Daoism, when the practitioner's *xing* is being explored, she or he is able to refine *jing* into qi (to a female, to refine fluid into *jing*); qi into *shen*, and to unify *jing*, qi and *shen* to the utmost integration, that is, change it back to the state of cosmic qi, a high level that a qigong practitioner can achieve (or refine qi into *shen* and back to the Cosmos, the origin). Now let's see how the theory of *xing* is established. First, let's see how the theory is expressed in this written character.

Xing 性 is pronounced using the falling tone. The written character of *xing* (nature) is formed by a part used as *xin* (heart+mind) and "alive, produce." When *xing* is used in the Chinese language it can be used in different ways to mean different things. It can mean either the sexual act of sex or the sex (gender) of male or female.

When the word *xing* is used in qigong, it is defined as "the original being"; in Daoist terms, *xing* is "the prenatal *shen*"; in Buddhist terms, it is called "the wisdom light." The term of *wuji*, also used in Confucianism, refers to "*xing*." (*Wuji* means infinite; the origin of yin and yang or called taiji). In the dictionary *xing* is translated into English as nature. We may call *xing* a person's spirit. According to any of these definitions, *xing* is not simply a soul.

Xing has no sex differences, never becomes ill, never ages, and is as eternal as the universe. This is why *xing*, the "origin," within any person is the same and perfect; and why *xing* has healing and paranormal powers.

We all in fact have our experiences of being close to our own *xing*s, such as when we get an inspiration. When you say "calm down" to an angry person, or "sleep on it and make the decision the next morning," you are giving advice to the person to let him or herself get in touch with her own being so that their wise inner spirits will be in charge and not the human mind. When a qigong teacher tells the students "to take a deep, thorough, soft, long breath, all the way down to the lower Dantian," this, in fact, is asking the students to take their minds down from the head and connect to their own beings with the help of breathing. When you are "just being" very relaxed and totally carefree, you are your original being. In the blank space between your two thoughts, you are your original being. This is why the longer you stay in this void state with the tiny bit of awareness in your heart, the longer you have to become your real self. To be able to stay in this state more often the biological body will begin to heal and aging slows down.

The erudite Daoist guru Chen Yingning defined *xing* a half century ago as:

"*Xing* and life belong to one originally and you cannot separate them into two. Such as the brainwave that is a sudden inspiration is from the *xing*; being vital is life. Our body is like a lamp, the lamp oil is the life; the *xing* gives off light. Without the lamp container holding the oil inside there will be no light. So you know without life, there will no show of *xing*. But if you only know to save the oil, but don't know how to light it to give off light, it will still be a dark world. Then what is the value of having a lamp with oil in it? From this you can tell *xing* and life are inseparable and mutually used. However, a human being cannot be called *xing*, neither can a life, just as the lamp container cannot be called oil, nor can the oil be called light. But to a beginner, life is more important... However, when reaching the highest level, *xing* is qi; qi is *xing*."

Self *xing* is radiance that the practitioner can see only in her/his void state of meditation. How much closer a qigong practitioner is to her or his own *xing* depends on self effort.

Qi Culture and Its Religions

I have met some people who confused qigong practice with a pure religion. Even a good healer can confuse qigong healing with a religious belief. Once I met a lady who had been a healer for over ten years and practices qigong. She believed that everything that happened had a reason that it was meant to happen thus there was no need to fight for a change. This is a misunderstanding about the practices of Daoism and qigong, also about the religion of Buddhism. Their essential teachings all are about how to make effort to change self fate. Old Monk Yun Gu (1500 – 1575) wrote,

"Fate cannot control a very good-hearted person, nor can it control a very evil person. Fate controls only the fates of ordinary people."

This philosophy of self-effort, shared by both Daoism, Buddhism, and qi practice, is told in the Chinese characters. For example the term for meditation, *da zuo* 打 坐, meaning to sit with legs crossed. *Da* 打 means "to do things with effort," such as *da gu*—beating a drum; *da tie*—forging iron; *da shui*—fetching water; *da majiang*— playing Mahjong; *da qiu*—playing ball; *da ren*—beating a person. The left side of *da* 打, is called, hand-side; the right side is 丁 "nail." Its written tells the "job" needs effort. *Zuo* 坐 means "to sit." 坐 is formed by two small persons, 人 on and separated by earth 土. 坐 hints deeper meaning in spiritual practice. So *da zuo*—to meditate needs lots of practice and to cross the legs can be painful in the beginning. Comparatively, to sit with legs crossed is easier to calm the qi energy and *xin* (heart and mind).

The second example of self-effort is "to pray," *qi dao* 祈祷. The two characters, *qi* 祈 is a different word from the qi energy 氣; *dao* 祷 is a different character from the word Dao 道. On their left sides both characters use a word, meaning "to show," to indicate personal effort, etc. I'll skip the rest of the character definitions. A good understanding of the qi practice will be beneficial. Otherwise the practitioner could be like the healer who I mentioned previously.

The various self-effort teachings are widely present in qigong theory because self-effort is the kernel power. Indeed, this culture has accumulated countless treasures for humankind. All the lineages handed down cultivations and practices, including both the religions of Daoism and Buddhism. All the lineages that passed on how to cultivate the human *xin* were all from "a big mercury ball that dropped in a plate, formed into small round balls, and into different sizes..." commented by a well known master Yuan Huanxian (a wealthy and well known Buddhist and Confucian guru in the 1930s. Buddhist expert and master Nan Huaijin is his disciple). He continued, "When someone truly gains this (understanding about the world truth), this'll be like to suddenly knock off the bottom of the bucket (see through now)!" Yuan Huanxian gave up all his wealth when he attained the Dao.

Although this energy has different names in Daoism and Buddhism, both consider this qi the base of life and the body and qi can be cultivated to heal. When tracing the essence of Buddhism, Daoism, and Confucianism, this helps to see their different ideas and methodologies mingling and aiming in the same direction. Both Buddhism and Daoism have branched into different styles, mainly are for purifying qi energy and heart and mind, including the practitioners who are not in a temple. And, in all the lineage practices incantations are involved. The sounds can also function purifying the qi energy; and the words ease the mind energy.

Both religions have their own natural "mummies" created by the high level masters themselves in China. They were delivered by self refining their qi. Both have masters who are able to show their body auras, just like the radiating auras around the sages' heads and bodies in the temple paintings. Also, they share the beliefs of reincarnation, afterlife, and karma, and both have records about masters who remember their previous lives.

Why has self-effort work on the qi and *xin* become the principle of any lineage and every person's cultivation? This is told in the sage's teaching:

"Dao implants great wisdom but self-knowledge is individually different."

The difference between us is mainly the *xin*. All practices handed down by the lineages request *xin* cultivation because no practitioner can advance unless she or he can "conquer" self *xin*. This is because human *xin*, or mind, is impulsive and contaminates qi. All our emotions, feelings, and thoughts do not belong to self-Heavenly *xin*— the true divine self. In Immortal Zhang Sanfeng's word:

"When the human *xin* is removed the Heavenly *xin* resides."

To end this introduction, I share with you what the ancient adepts constantly reminded the cultivators and the common readers: "When using language to guide people, the explanation of Dao is limited by the language." There is a Chinese idiom, *xin ling shen hui* 心领神会, indicating this key way of learning. Although this idiom is often translated and understood as "hint," yet it means much more. So I translate it word by word, "When (two person's) *xin*s understand (each other), the spirits meet." Or, just by the words: *xin*, guides/leads, spirit(s), meet. This is an unspoken understanding and is what I hope the reader gains in this book and in this introduction, and all the books alike.

Generally, in today's busy life if one can sit to empty all the thoughts and meditate for about 30 minutes, this can help him or her mind become clear and improve both work and life. And a qi practitioner always looks younger than other people their age. In order to do better, a brief self-education can be quite helpful. However, when the practitioner is interested in pursuing more, he or she will need to educate self first and find a qualified teacher. And, to have faith in self is important.

Yanling Johnson
July 2011

QUESTIONS AND ANSWERS ABOUT JINGGONG (QUIET MEDITATION EXERCISE) THERAPY FOR STRESS-RELATED DISORDERS

By Chen Yingning
Translated by Yang Shuhui and Yang Yunqin

CONTENTS

This article was written by Mr. Chen Yingning in August 1957 during his sojourn as a guest lecturer at the Screen Hill Sanatorium in Hangzhou, Zhejiang province. After revisions by the author himself, the article was published in the No. 3 issue of the Journal of the Daoist Association, *1963.*

Introduction

All illnesses and diseases are treatable by medication, surgery, or physical therapy. Most are curable. The exceptions are cancer, mankind's bane for which there is no complete cure by Chinese or Western medicine, and stress-related disorders which, although less life-threatening than cancer, baffle the average physician. This is an ailment common to those engaged in mentally challenging jobs. Nerves constitute the essence of life. Applying medicine to fortify nerves that had already been weakened by stress is not likely to produce the desired effect. Only Jinggong in its purest form is the best remedy for frayed nerves, remedy that leads to healing without the intervention of medicine.

I consider myself fortunate in that what little service I have rendered to the newly-established Jinggong Therapy Department of the Screen Hill Sanatorium during my recent stay there was successful. Since I could not stay there for too long, I planned to produce a manuscript complete with theory and specific instructions for the benefit of my successors. However, given the pressure of time, which does not allow a leisurely systematic narration chapter after chapter, I settled for a question-and-answer format

Questions and Answers about Jinggong
(Quiet Meditation Exercise)
Therapy for Stress-related Disorders

in which I deal with the topics one by one as I go along. (The entries include conversations I have had with physicians and patients at the sanatorium.) This being a newly established discipline with no precedents or reference books to fall back on, nor anyone to consult with, since medical researchers do not engage in practice and those who do have no interest in seeking medical knowledge, everything I say is based on my experience for more than sixty years, not from teachers or colleagues (what I said about the dearth of reference books and people to consult with does not apply to post-1957 years). Twenty-seven questions and answers, plus an article presenting general theories on Jinggong and an article on treatment of involuntary nocturnal emission, should suffice to tackle with stress-related disorders.

This being no more than a first draft, I expect to have the inadequacies in understanding, methodology, and diction remedied in a second edition.

Chen Yingning

August 1957

Workers' Sanatorium, Screen Hill, Hangzhou

Questions and Answers about Jinggong

1. Question: Is Jinggong one and the same with Qigong?

Answer: The focus of Jinggong is on *jing* (quiet, calm), not on qi (vital energy), whereas the focus of Qigong is on qi. Qigong exercises involve motions. They are not stationary. There is a whole array of different Qigong exercises taught all over the world—exercises on deep-breathing, reverse breathing, breath counting, breath adjustment, breath retention, and qi movements. There are also breathing techniques of frontal elevation and rear descent, rear elevation and frontal descent, left-to-right rotations and middle-section direct penetration, etc. All of the above-mentioned exercises involve qi, whereas Jinggong is done in complete stillness, with natural breathing. No effort is made to force the direction of the qi of the body. Otherwise, the word *jing* (quiet, calm) would lose its meaning.

2. Question: What are the advantages and disadvantages of Jinggong as compared to Qigong?

Answer: If done properly, Qigong can cure all illnesses but if not, it will not only fail to cure, but also add new illnesses to your body. As for Jinggong, if done properly, of course it cures all diseases that resist medicine but even if it is not done properly, it still brings benefit to the body.

Questions and Answers about Jinggong
(Quiet Meditation Exercise)
Therapy for Stress-related Disorders

At least it will surely not bring on new illnesses even if it produces no effect. Therefore, Qigong has advantages and disadvantages but Jinggong has only advantages.

3. Question: What kinds of people can do Qigong?

Answer: If you are a flexible person smart enough to stop immediately whatever you think you are not doing right and even to shift to another mode to deal with the situation, you are the right person to do Qigong. But those without much good sense, those prone to stubbornly digging in their heels even if they are not doing it right, should not do Qigong because they will not know how to respond to unexpected changes in the body. They will only do harm to their own health.

4. Question: What kinds of people can do Jinggong?

Answer: Everyone, male or female, old or young, smart or not, can do it. Those who are impulsive and restless may not enjoy it, but if they are willing to do it, they should also be able to achieve good results, although, in their case, it may take longer for results to show than in the case of those of a quiet disposition.

5. Question: What kinds of illnesses respond well to Qigong treatment?

Answer: According to theories of Chinese medicine, the following kinds of patients respond well to medication as well as to Qigong: those susceptible to colds and coughs due to a deficiency of qi in the lungs; those with poor appetite and indigestion due to stomach qi deficiency, those whose three visceral cavities housing the internal organs are blocked due to retention of dampness or phlegm and are therefore vulnerable to all kinds of illnesses; those whose intestines absorb water poorly or whose with unformed stool due to deficiency of qi in the body cavity between the diaphragm and the umbilicus housing the spleen; those with excessive urine that is clear and cloudy by turns due to kidney qi deficiency; those lacking energy due to liver qi deficiency; and those with problems of metabolism, in the language of Western medicine.

6. Question: What are the illnesses that Jinggong works best on?

Answer: All illnesses that arise from a weakened constitution. Symptoms include: dizziness, lightheadedness, blurred vision, ringing in the ears, palpitation, panic attacks, insomnia, nightmares, restlessness, edginess, crankiness, dejection, overanxiety, moodiness, forgetfulness, weakness in the legs, loss of muscle, malnutrition due to insufficient food intake, indigestion due to overeating,

Questions and Answers about Jinggong
(Quiet Meditation Exercise)
Therapy for Stress-related Disorders

little tolerance for hard work, and lack of interest in life. Medication rarely relieves these symptoms and physical exams fail to pinpoint the problem. The only cure is in Jinggong. For quicker results, Jinggong can be combined with exercises such as taiji (taichi) or calisthenics.

7. Question: The ordinary Quiet Sitting Therapy is inseparable from Qigong. Why do you draw a distinction between Jinggong and Qigong?

Answer: Jinggong is focused on stillness and Qigong on motion. So they are different in nature. The ordinary Quiet Sitting Therapy is not in line with the principles of Jinggong. Those who practice the Quiet Sitting Therapy may be sitting immobile, but their minds are still alert. Despite its name, it's a therapy that involves motion and therefore does not qualify as real Jinggong.

8. Question: What qualifies as Jinggong?

Answer: Step 1: Keep your body still. Step 2: Keep your mind still. Step 3: Tune out all thoughts about your body. Forget that "I" exists.

9. Question: What is so good about reaching such a state?

Answer: The human body has the built-in strength to fight diseases, but a weakened constitution or other obstacles block it. Jinggong's role is to help the body eliminate the obstacles and regain its own innate strength. Once the strength is brought out, healing will only be a matter of time.

10. Question: How does one go about the three steps?

Answer: Whether sitting or lying flat, you start by relaxing until there is no tense spot throughout your body and you feel completely at ease. If you do it right, you will not feel bored with the lapse of time, nor will you feel pain or numbness. This means that your body has achieved peace, but your mind may still be disturbed. So the next step is to banish all thoughts from your mind. Do not think of the past, the present, or the future. Let your mind enjoy complete rest. Now, even though your mind gains peace, you may still be conscious of yourself. So the next step is to enter a drowsy, dreamless state in which you are not aware of anything, not even of your own existence. If you have dreams, that means your mind is still at work. Your emotions—joy, anger, sadness, fear—and your thoughts about food, drink, and sex can be kept under control when you are sober but not when you are in dreamland. If you are in such a state, you are not completely free from self-consciousness.

11. Question: When sitting still, one's body may sud-

Questions and Answers about Jinggong
(Quiet Meditation Exercise)
Therapy for Stress-related Disorders

denly stir involuntarily, and the movements vary from person to person, even in the same person. These movements are quite outside of one's control. What are the reasons for such a strange phenomenon?

Answer: This is caused by the vital energy of the human body. If this is strange, what would you say about the numerous other strange things in the human body? There is the breathing of the lungs, the palpitations of the heart, the peristalsis of the stomach and the intestines, the digestion of food, the excretion of the glands, the metabolism of cells, the growth of hair and nails, the union of sperm and ovum, and the formation of a fetus. Which one of those is under the control of one's mind? If you are not surprised at all these mysterious, imperceptible workings inside the body, why should you be surprised at involuntary external movements?

12. Question: The workings inside the body have never been controllable since birth and it's the same for everybody. That's why we don't find them surprising. But external movements have always followed the directions of the mind. And if, all of a sudden, you start to have these involuntary movements, won't you worry that things will eventually get out of hand? How strange you would look if you are always shaking your limbs and jerking your head! Are there ways to keep the movements under control?

Answer: As long as you do Jinggong right, breathe normally, and do not force your body movements the way you do calisthenics, no harm will be done. Any involuntary movements will stop by themselves with the passage of time. If you lose patience and want them to stop immediately, that can also be done. You just need to put a stop to Jinggong, let your mind wander, and even exercise a little control, and the movements will stop. But the principle of Jinggong is the absence of motion. Movements are the exceptions. Do not believe that movements are unavoidable for all those practicing Jinggong.

13. Question: Is it true that after the first time, such involuntary movements will become habitual every time you do Jinggong?

Answer: No. After all the qi in your body and your limbs can flow freely and unobstructed, no involuntary movements will occur during your Jinggong sessions. Even so, the qi under your navel may inevitably move around. You should know this, so that you won't panic when this happens. If you don't know how to respond, you will only make matters worse.

Questions and Answers about Jinggong
(Quiet Meditation Exercise)
Therapy for Stress-related Disorders

14. Question: How are such involuntary movements during a Jinggong session related to therapy?

Answer: Some illnesses are obvious to the patient and the physician, some are hidden. In fact, they can be so deeply hidden that no tests can pick them up. After you become quite accomplished in your Jinggong skills, the vital energy in your body will be unleashed, so that if an illness blocks its way, it will put up a fight, causing your limbs and joints to jerk involuntarily. After several sessions, some of the obstacles will be removed, but the remaining ones will make you involuntarily jerk in other ways. By the time all obstacles have been gradually gotten out of the way, you will have no involuntary movements in your Jinggong sessions.

15. Question: If these movements are soft and gentle, it's all right not to do anything about them but to let them subside on their own. However, if the movements are too violent, to the point where you flail your arms and legs around non-stop, what are you going to do?

Answer: This has to do with the patient's constitution. If Jinggong works well on you, that means your constitution is very likely a weak one, and therefore you are definitely not prone to violent movements. If you have a strong constitution and just happen to be slightly ill, you can just take the right medication for it rather than practicing Jinggong. So you need not worry on that score. Now, if the involuntary movements are due to the fact that the patient's constitution is not one for Jinggong, and the Jinggong is not done in the right way, then the instructor should make adjustments and try to stop the movements before selecting other methods suitable for the patient. The idea is not to rush things.

16. Question: Will involuntary movements happen to everyone practicing Jinggong?

Answer: No. Most people engaged in Jinggong do not have such movements.

17. Question: Doesn't everybody practice the same Jinggong? Why are some people immune?

Answer: That's because everybody's constitution is different. That's why the same medication for the same illness can produce different results.

18. Question: Are involuntary movements good or bad according to the principles of Jinggong?

Answer: Many ancient books on cultivation of the body talk only about vibrations inside the body while sitting still. No mention is made of external involuntary move-

Questions and Answers about Jinggong
(Quiet Meditation Exercise)
Therapy for Stress-related Disorders

ments. Those practicing Jinggong in those times made it a rule that the body should not move. If limb movements occurred, the instructor would reproach the student for having committed a cardinal mistake and try to set him/her straight. However, of the many cases of involuntary movements I have witnessed over the last few decades, the results are mixed. It's hard to generalize. As I see it, the purpose of practicing Jinggong being to cure illnesses, if a patient regains health, we'll say the therapy worked; if not, we'll say it failed. If the movements make you feel good, we'll say Jinggong is effective on you; if not, we'll say it doesn't work for you. So do not pass judgments on the effectiveness of Jinggong just by the occurrence or absence of involuntary movements.

19. Question: I understand that there is supposed to be movements of qi in the abdomen in a properly done Jinggong session. Is it true that such qi movements occur only after the phase of external involuntary movements is over?

Answer: Not necessarily. (1) A small number of people engaged in Jinggong feel movements of qi in the abdomen toward the end of the phase of external movements. (2) Some people experience no abdominal movements even after the phase of external movements is over. For them, abdominal qi movements begin to occur only after they go through a phase of complete stillness. (3) There are also people who skip the stage of involuntary movements. Their accomplishment is such that they feel warm qi surging in the abdomen. (4) A majority of people experience no unusual conditions in years of Jinggong practice, but their weak constitution gradually regains health without their realizing it. So, for those engaged in Jinggong, involuntary external or internal movements or the lack of them or their sequence can vary from person to person. There is no fixed pattern.

20. Question: When one becomes quite accomplished in Jinggong, what should be done if there is internal surging of qi but no external movements?

Answer: When this happens, just remain still and let the qi run its own course. You need only be slightly conscious of the qi. Do not, on any account, try to help it, direct it, or suppress it. Just slowly and gradually let it go away and stop on its own. After you regain your normal state, you can sit still for another 30 minutes before leaving your seat. When the moving qi has not yet come to a complete stop, do not abruptly end your Jinggong session, and allow yourself to be alarmed, disturbed, have troubled thoughts, or get angry. Otherwise, things may go wrong.

Questions and Answers about Jinggong
(Quiet Meditation Exercise)
Therapy for Stress-related Disorders

21. Question: Could you explain the therapeutic effect of Jinggong in the light of modern medical science?

Answer: Jinggong's origin predates the Qin Dynasty (221 – 206 BC). It sprang from Daoist roots, not from the medical profession. Moreover, physicians of the successive dynasties never used Jinggong to cure illnesses. Chao Yu-anfang, celebrated physician of the Sui Dynasty (581 – 618), advocated in *The Origins of Diseases* various methods of guiding the qi to cure all kinds of illnesses, but these methods all involve willful movements and therefore do not qualify as Jinggong. So, no theoretical base is to be found in writings on traditional Chinese medicine, let alone Western medical literature. However, after Pavlov's theory became public knowledge, most of the reasons for Jinggong treatment became explainable. In short, the basic idea was to rid the higher nerve center of all impairments and restore its normal function. However, some exceptional phenomena in the entire process of Jinggong practice still defy explanation. Our job is to use our ancestors' methods to our advantage and help physicians of today treat stress-related disorders. The exceptional phenomena can be ignored for now and left for future studies.

22. Question: Does Jinggong, as you call it, go by other names in ancient books on self-cultivation?

Answer: It's called *zuo wang* (sit in oblivion) in Tang Dynasty (618 – 907) books and *zhi nian* (stop all thoughts) in Song Dynasty (960 – 1279) books. They are similar to what I call Jinggong in theory, but not in purpose. Our purpose is to cure illnesses; theirs is to cultivate body and mind. But in *Collections of All Books Past and Present*, there is a chapter devoted to Jinggong, in which the instructions are extremely complex. They are by no means for pure Jinggong, so students should avoid being confused by the identical name. (The chapter on Jinggong referred to above is in Volumes 293 – 302 in the part on the supernatural in the *Encyclopedia of Natural Sciences*.)

23. Question: In books of antiquity, what is the name for Qigong as we know it now?

Answer: What is now practiced widely today as Qigong is a combination of exhalation, inhalation, breath retention, breath adjustment, relaxation of mind, and guidance of qi, etc., as advocated by the sages. Exhalation and inhalation mean exhaling through the mouth the old and stagnant air in the lungs and inhaling clean air through the nose. Breath retention means holding the fresh air in the lungs for a while after inhaling. Breath adjustment means that breathing should proceed from harsh to gentle, from hard to soft, from quick to slow, and from shal-

Questions and Answers about Jinggong
(Quiet Meditation Exercise)
Therapy for Stress-related Disorders

low to deep, but this should happen naturally, in stages. Do not force things. Relaxation of mind means focusing the mind on one fixed spot in the body so as to banish all other thoughts from your mind. Guidance of qi means that when you are accomplished enough to feel warm qi moving in your lower abdomen, be sure to let your mind guide the qi throughout the body to drive away illnesses, if any, or simply, in the absence of illnesses, to build up your health. But this is different from what is practiced by kung fu masters and by those practicing the Daoist "cinnabar field" (lower abdomen) methods of breathing. So beginners must take care not to mix them up. There is a host of other techniques of directing the qi: the Five-fowl Method of Hua Tuo (physician, ? – 208), the Eight-section Qigong Exercises (Ba Duan Jin), the Twelve-section Qigong Exercises (Shi Er Duan Jin), the Daoist method for Muscle Change Classic, and the many other exercises described in *The Origins of Diseases* written by physicians of the Sui Dynasty. They are all methods to direct the qi. (Methods practiced by kung fu masters, Daoists, and Buddhists are now all lumped together under the term Qigong, making it sound extremely complicated.)

24. Question: Since there are so many kinds of Qigong, each must have its own advantages in treating illnesses.

By leaving aside Qigong and fo cusing on Jinggong only, aren't you being one-sided?

Answer: I do so after careful considerations. I have my reasons.

(1) With other ways of treating illnesses (like medicine, physical therapy), however complicated they may be, the patient leaves everything to the doctors and nurses, and doesn't get consumed with worry. But in the case of Qigong, patients have to do it themselves. No one can do it for them. Some patients do not want to take the trouble. Some are willing to do it, but few get the hang of it. One must pick the simplest and most effective method out of the multitudes of available methods to make it more easily acceptable to patients. That is why I chose the simplest way out and put my focus on Jinggong.

(2) With regard to movements of taiji or other similar exercises, not everybody can do them properly even when there are illustrations to consult and instructors' demonstrations to imitate. Since Qigong involves what happens inside the body, illustrations can't capture it and instructors can't demonstrate for you, so patients have to be responsible for themselves. Some people get the hang of it, and some don't. It is in order to be on the safe side that I chose to concentrate on Jinggong today rather than on Qigong.

(3) For better results, all treatments of illnesses must be supplemented by Jinggong and Qigong. In the çase of

Questions and Answers about Jinggong
(Quiet Meditation Exercise)
Therapy for Stress-related Disorders

stomach ulcer, Qigong alone, without the involvement of Jinggong, can hardly do much good, but Jinggong alone, without Qigong, can heal ulcers. This has been borne out by my own experience more than once. In fact, those recent much-celebrated cases of successful Qigong therapies all contain some elements of Jinggong in them and, what's more, it's the Jinggong elements that played a major role. After regaining health, patients all attribute the success to Qigong, whereas, in fact, Jinggong was quietly doing its stuff, and Qigong only played a supplementary role. That is why I chose to concentrate on Jinggong.

(4) With conventional treatments, the physicians make all the decisions for the patients. It follows that the physicians are responsible for all successes or failures. But as far as Qigong is concerned, it's the patient who takes the initiative. The physician's role is limited to providing a few pointers. If the exercises are not done properly and result in health disturbances, thus diminishing the effectiveness of the therapy, the doctor and the patient will put the blame on each other. Who should be held accountable for the mistakes? Jinggong is easier for beginners than Qigong. Even if no quick fix can be managed, at least nothing can go wrong. After explaining Jinggong to in-patients, the instructor can let them practice on their own. It will be enough for the instructor to check the pa-

tients twice a day rather than keep them under constant observance. To train Jinggong students is obviously easier and simpler than to train Qigong students. That is also why I chose to concentrate on Jinggong.

(5) In this day and age, most chronic diseases can probably be attributed to weakened constitutions. If properly diagnosed, some can be treated with medicine prescribed to match the disorder. For example, weakened digestive functions can be treated with tonics for the stomach, weakened reproduction functions with hormone therapies, weakened hematogenic functions with blood tonics, weakened metabolic functions with tonics to nourish the qi. These are all effective treatments. However, there are no effective cures, in Chinese or Western medicine, for weakened constitutions caused by stress or other factors not listed above. The only treatment in such cases is for the patient to rest thoroughly in complete calmness for an extended period of time. Because no Qigong exercises fit this principle, I chose to focus on Jinggong.

(6) Peace is what's lacking in people's lives. In the twenty-four hour cycle, the limbs may have moments of rest, but the mind never enjoys peace. It works when you are awake and is disturbed by dreams when you are asleep, and you feel just as tired in your dreams as when awake. Years of mental exhaustion will result in nervous

Questions and Answers about Jinggong
(Quiet Meditation Exercise)
Therapy for Stress-related Disorders

breakdown. Healthy people who take time out from their busy schedule to do Jinggong twice a day will be able, if they keep at it, to prevent nervous breakdowns and prolong life. That is another reason why I chose to concentrate on Jinggong.

(7) As for what kinds of Qigong are advisable for what illnesses and what kinds of illnesses should not be treated by Qigong, there are no simple answers. Decisions must be made in the light of theory as well as clinical experience. An instructor's job is by no means easy. Even if the instructor is not at fault, the patient may do it wrong and go overboard, which is why Qigong-induced health disturbances are only to be expected. Jinggong, on the other hand, is applicable to everyone and every kind of illness. You need not worry about matching the exercise to the illness. Instructors can not go wrong, and students can't overdo it. One almost never hears about cases of Jinggong practices going awry. Another reason why I opted for Jinggong.

(8) My focus on Jinggong doesn't mean a blanket condemnation of all kinds of Qigong. If the instructor is knowledgeable in the advantages and disadvantages of various kinds of Qigong and gains a clear idea of the patient's constitution and character, he may choose one particular kind of Qigong for the patient on an ad-hoc

basis. This will work better on patients with complicated stress-related disorders, with Jinggong playing a major role and Qigong a supplementary one.

25. Question: What are the qualifications for an instructor?

Answer: In the old days, there was nothing challenging about the instructor's job. Having the students memorize a rhymed formula was all it took. It was up to the students themselves to try to get the hang of it through practice. The instructor was not accountable for success or failure, and the students had no expectations of an immediate cure because their hopes lay elsewhere. They did not expect to be cured in the first place, and not every student was sick. But nowadays, since all those checked into a sanatorium expect to be cured, the instructor doubles as a physician, and this makes the job much more demanding. So the qualifications of an instructor include: (1) Medical knowledge. (2) Clinical experience. (3) A gentle disposition and therefore not likely to find patients a nuisance. (4) A willingness to listen and not to hold on to preconceived ideas. (5) The ability to prevent errors on the part of the patients and to correct them if this happens. (6) The ability to tell if some irregularities experienced by a patient mean trouble or not and to teach the patient to deal with them. Inner exercises (including Buddhist and

Questions and Answers about Jinggong
(Quiet Meditation Exercise)
Therapy for Stress-related Disorders

Daoist Jinggong and all varieties of Qigong) used to circulate among a small minority of people. They have never
been, as they are now, taken up by sanatoriums all over
the country as a therapy. This is a new undertaking. Today's instructors can hardly stand a chance if they have
no knowledge of the old ways, but if they only know the
old ways and lack other branches of knowledge, they also
fall short of the requirements for the job in this day and
age. A qualified instructor is one who meets the above-
cited requirements and never stops learning to master all
methods, achieve a thorough understanding, accumulate
experience, and apply his expertise with flexibility.

26. Question: What should one watch out for before
starting Jinggong sessions?

Answer: In order to achieve quick results, directors of
sanatoriums and patients themselves should watch out for
the following ten things:

(1) The noise level of the surrounding environment.
Those practicing Jinggong must first pick the right location.
The most ideal location is a spot on a wooded hill or by a
body of water. The next best is a quiet place in an open coun-
tryside. Markets, alleys, and all other places with high noise
levels won't do. Human voice, the rumbling of wheels, the
throbbing of engines, music, singing, babies' cries—these

should all be avoided to give your ears some peace and quiet rather than irritate your audio nerves.

(2) The quality of the air. The air around you should be very fresh and clean, without dust, exhaust from cars, and all kinds of foul smell, like those from gasoline, kitchen odors, paint, mosquito-repellent incense, disinfectants, etc. They all do harm. Indoor furniture should be kept only at a minimum. Too many objects are also likely to emit unpleasant odor. The air in a place with lush green plants is beneficial to health, and gives your nose some peace and quiet so that your olfactory nerves will not be irritated.

(3) The lighting. With regard to indoor lighting, seekers of health in ancient times emphasized the balance of yin and yang so that one would not overwhelm the other. So it is advisable not to be too bright or too dark. Since our purpose is to heal, we need to make sure that our nerves are absolutely at peace without any irritation. Excessive light is worse than darkness. So it would be best to have light blue or light green wall paint and curtains. Avoid bright red or white. Electric lighting should not be glaring. Rid the room of eyesores, and also make sure that nothing outside the window offends the eye. This is to give peace to your eyes so that nothing irritates your visual nerves.

(4) Food seasoning. Food should not be overly pun-

Questions and Answers about Jinggong
(Quiet Meditation Exercise)
Therapy for Stress-related Disorders

gent, sweet, sour, salty, or spicy hot. The more bland the better. Do more boiling and steaming than braising in soy sauce and frying. What pleases your taste buds too much may not be good for you. Also, give up smoking and drinking alcohol. This is to give peace to your tongue so that your sense of taste will not be irritated.

(5) The climate. Temperature has a great impact on Jinggong practice. Good weather will help you make progress with your exercises. Bad weather will be a hindrance. When it is so hot that you sweat even though you are wearing only one layer of clothing, when it is so cold that you don't feel warm even though you have a cotton-padded coat on, and when humidity is too high, your exercises will hardly be effective. If a rainstorm comes on with claps of thunder and flashes of lightning, you must stop your Jinggong session. If it warms up when you are in the middle of a session, do not turn on the electric fan. If it gets cold, do not light a fire (central heating is OK). Some people say that a chimney is not harmful. This doesn't make sense from a scientific perspective. Granted that the advantage of a chimney is to release the carbon dioxide from the fuel, but it also has a disadvantage: It consumes oxygen contained in the air in the room. A low oxygen level is injurious to even a healthy person, let alone a sick one. If it is necessary to use a chimney, see to it that the

doors and windows are not tightly closed. You must let in some air from outside. Make sure that while there is circulation of air in the room, the patient should be kept from whiffs of cold air, to avoid catching cold. In general, good weather lasts less than six months out of a year. If it's nice today, it may change for the worse tomorrow. Jinggong devotees are advised to seize the moment when the climate is right.

(6) Food nutrition. Foods high in protein do nourish the body but they need to be digested well. Otherwise, excessive intake of such foods is harmful. People with frayed nerves usually also have digestion problems. So, high-protein foods should be taken in moderation. That applies also to dietary supplements. Junk foods must be banned. Do not satisfy your cravings at the expense of your health.

(7) Suspension of all ties with the outside world. Of course you are expected to put your job on hold for the entire duration of your stay in the sanatorium for Jinggong therapy, but your private matters and everything involving your family must also be planned out in advance to spare you worries. Once you have checked into the sanatorium, keep visits from relatives and friends at a minimum; reduce all exposure to the outside world by limiting your phone calls, newspaper reading, and letter writing. You will then be able to stay calm and find it

Questions and Answers about Jinggong
(Quiet Meditation Exercise)
Therapy for Stress-related Disorders

easier to learn Jinggong and speed up the healing process.

(8) Keep your mind unoccupied. I advise against reading books that require mental application, especially science literature with complex math formulas and numbers. If you enjoy reading for amusement, it's all right to leaf through magazines and travel books. During Jinggong sessions, focus your mind on listening to your breathing. When taking a walk, focus your mind on the flowers, grass, trees, hills, and waters. During a meal, focus your mind on the presentation, smell, and taste of the food (sanatoriums should take seriously the presentation, smell, and taste of the food they serve). When doing calisthenics or taiji, focus your mind on your limb movements.

(9) The timing of exercise. Jinggong can be done at all times of the day, although morning is best. A sitting session should last at least 30 minutes but less than 90 minutes. A lie-in-bed session has no limits of time. You can lie for as long as you want. It would be best if you can sleep throughout the night without waking up even once. If you wake up in the night and toss and turn, wide awake, you may get up and do a sitting session until you get so sleepy that you have to lie down again. This is a sure-fire way to drop off to sound sleep. However, do not start a sitting session or go to sleep right after a big meal, before digestion sets in. You need to exercise a little first.

(10) The posture. The principle of Jinggong being thorough mental physical rest, posture is not important. You can sit with your legs crossed or dangling, lie on your back or on your side, with both eyes fully or partially closed, hands crossed or apart, palms up or down. But it's stricter with the sitting posture. You must sit with your back straight. Do not slouch, but do not force it. There must be nothing around you that you can lean against. When lying down, your head should be higher than your feet in a progressively downward slant. Do not use a high pillow because that will only raise your head but cannot ensure a gradually reclining slant. It's preferable to use a hard bed. Slip something under the feet of the headboard of the bed and raise them by seven or eight inches. Leave the two feet at the other end untouched, so that the bed becomes tilted. But this method should not be applied to those suffering from cerebral anemia. Whether seated or in a supine position, the body must be totally relaxed. All restraining objects such as shoes and belts must be taken off, so that there is no restriction anywhere. This is the only way to ensure complete tranquility. In addition, all mosquitoes, bedbugs, and fleas must be exterminated. Even one or two of such pests can ruin your Jinggong session. All other details that I have not touched upon can be taken care of according to the general rules of the sanatoriums.

Questions and Answers about Jinggong
(Quiet Meditation Exercise)
Therapy for Stress-related Disorders

27. Question: Is it better to practice Jinggong in a group in a large room or by oneself in a small room?

Answer: There are pros and cons with both. It's hard to say which one is better. In a group setting, mutual observance may give inspiration but it may also give rise to self-consciousness. Doing it by oneself at one's own free will may make one feel isolated and become lazy. Buddhists who practice in shrine halls together follow the group method. Those who practice in thatched huts in remote mountains follow the individual method. Although their practice has purposes different from ours, their methods are of value to us. Modern sanatoriums preferably should provide both kinds of accommodations to patients, so that they can make their choices as needed.

A General Introduction to Jinggong

The above twenty-seven questions and answers covered matters relating to Jinggong from all possible angles, but there were not enough detailed instructions on the exercise itself. So here is some more information:

There is currently no effective medicine for stress-related disorders. Phosphoric supplements' claim to fortifying the brain is unsubstantiated. All other stimulants or sedatives have only temporary effect. After the effect wears out, the symptoms come back, maybe with a vengeance.

One must ensure complete tranquility of the mind and disperse all random thoughts from it. This is the most important principle of Jinggong practice and is the most effective treatment for stress-related disorders. However, it is difficult to put a stop to all the thoughts that go habitually through your mind. Our forefathers devised a host of methods to attain this purpose, among which the best one is Zhuangzi's "listen-to-breathing" method (Zhuangzi, c. 369 – 286 BC).

You begin this exercise by using only your ears, not your mind. The idea is not to replace one thought with another, but more to force yourself to stay vigilant about your nose or your lungs. Nor is it to listen to any nasal sound. As long as you are aware of the exhalations and the inhalations, you are doing it right. Do not try to control the speed and depth of the breathing. Just let them be. By and by, your breath will be at one with your qi. All distracting thoughts will vanish. You will even forget about your breathing and gradually drift off to sleep. This is the most opportune moment to restore vigor to your frayed nerves. Seize the moment and abandon yourself to deep sleep. Be sure not to resist the temptation to sleep. After you wake up, repeat the exercise all over again, and you will be able to drop off to blissful sleep again. If you have already slept several times during the day and do not

Questions and Answers about Jinggong
(Quiet Meditation Exercise)
Therapy for Stress-related Disorders

wish to sleep any more, you may get up and do some light exercise in a woody place outside where the air is fresh and clean. You may stand there for a few minutes doing breathing exercises, or practice calisthenics or taichi. But do not go overboard. Do not tire yourself out. Once you return indoors, you may either sit or lie in bed, resume your "listening-to-breathing" exercise and, perhaps, to fall asleep again.

Most people with stress-related disorders are also plagued by insomnia. It is not advisable to take sleep pills on a regular basis. Only the "listening-to-breathing" method can tackle the problem at the root, without leaving any side effect. It is in keeping with the theory about yang entering yin in the *Classic of Internal Medicine* (*Huang Di Nei Jing*, China's earliest work on medicine completed between 770 BC – 25 AD).

Ancient books on medicine often make reference to the interdependence of the mind and the breath, but no specific instructions can be found. Su Dongpo's way is to count your breathings and then let the mind follow the breath (Su Dongpo, 1037 – 1101, a famous Chinese poet). Zhu Xi's way, as explained in his *Advice on Breath Adjustment*, is to "watch the tip of your nose," according to *The Surangama Sutra* (Zhu Xi, 1130 – 1200, Confucian scholar and founder of the school of Neo-Confucianism). However, since you have to count, you are not free from all engagement of the mind. And, in the latter case, since you have to watch your nose, your eyes will get tired over time. Zhuangzi's "listening-to-breathing" method is the only one that calls for absolutely no engagement of the mind and leads to no fatigue. What follows is a list of the three methods for you to practice.

1. Su Dongpo's Theory on Health (*Dongpo Zhilin, Su Shi's Record in His Daily Life,* Vol.1)

Health conscious people must exercise moderation in their eating habits. Only when plagued with hunger can you start eating and you should stop before the feeling of fullness sets in. After each meal, take a stroll outdoors until the food has been digested. Then return indoors for exercises. You can freely decide whether to do the exercises in daytime or at night, seated or lying down. The only important thing is to keep your body from moving and stay immobile like a wooden statue. Then, in a combination of Buddhist and Daoist methods, gaze at the tip of your own nose while counting the number of exhalations and inhalations through your nose. The key is to empty your mind and not to force anything. When counting, count either all the exhalations or all the inhalations, not both. So each act of breathing, exhaling and inhaling, counts as one, not two. After you've counted hundreds of times, your mind will be a blank and your body motionless as a rock. Since you need not force anything on your mind and body, both will naturally enjoy tranquility.

Questions and Answers about Jinggong
(Quiet Meditation Exercise)
Therapy for Stress-related Disorders

After you've counted thousands of times, or if you have no more strength to go on counting, you can switch to another method, called "follow the breath." When you exhale, let your mind follow the air out of the body. When you inhale, let your mind follow the air on its way in, not through the nostrils, but filling every pore like evaporation of cloud and fog. When you attain this level of accomplishment, all long-standing ailments and afflictions will gradually go away and you reach enlightenment, just like a blind man suddenly regaining sight. Able to see his way ahead now, he no longer needs guidance.

2. Zhu Xi's Breath-Adjustment Method (*The Complete Works of Zhu Xi,* Vol. 85)

Watching the tip of one's own nose is the 14th of the 25 methods listed in *The Surangama Sutra*. Both Su Dongpo and Zhu Xi adopted the phrase, but each in a slightly different sense. In Zhu Xi's words, this is a method applicable anywhere and at any time, provided you are relaxed and feel comfortable. Do not make yourself uncomfortable in any way. Stay calm and let things take their own course. Do not force anything. When tranquility reaches its height, the pendulum will naturally swing toward motion, like fish rising to the surface of the water in spring to breathe. When motion reaches its height, the pendulum swings naturally toward tranquility, like insects hibernating in winter to conserve energy. At this point, the qi in the body converges with the qi of heaven and earth, and the alterations of tranquility and motion unite with the movements of the universe. Words are inadequate to describe the wonders of this method. You may ask, who is behind all this? In fact, there is no one behind any of this. Everything is just a part of nature.

3. The Mind Tranquility Method of Zhuangzi
(*Chapter IV, The Book of Zhuangzi*)

Yan Hui asked Confucius, his teacher, about Zhuangzi's Mind Tranquility method, and this was Confucius' reply: Do not indulge in wild fancies. Gather all your thoughts together and then listen, not with your ears but with your mind. Then, listen not with your mind but with your qi. By this time, you should no longer be relying on your ears. Your mind and qi being at one, you should not be relying on your mind, either. Qi is something unsubstantial. It needs something to form a union with it. Only Dao can merge with the qi of the Great Void. If your mind attains the tranquility of the Great Void, you have made a success of the Mind Tranquility method.

There should be no division of stages to this method, but for the convenience of beginners, I'm going to divide the whole process into several steps and give some detailed instructions:

Step 1: "Gather all your thoughts together." Before you

Questions and Answers about Jinggong
(Quiet Meditation Exercise)
Therapy for Stress-related Disorders

begin the exercise, be sure to gather all your thoughts together and concentrate on the exercise. If any distracting thoughts remain, you will not be able to do a good job of it.

Step 2: "Listen not with your ears but with your mind." Once you have completed Step 1, you are ready to begin to "listen," but definitely not to listen with your ears to conventional sounds. You may get skeptical and ask, since it involves listening, what am I supposed to listen to, if not to sounds? No clear answer to this question can be found in the annotations to all kinds of theories. So let me make this clear: You begin by listening for the sound of breathing through your nostrils. The breathing of those with normal, unimpeded respiratory systems should be noiseless, which is why you are not supposed to listen with your ears. Even though there is no sound, you are aware of the speed and the strength of exhalations and inhalations through the nostrils, as are even the hearing-impaired. That's why the instructions are to "listen with your mind."

Step 3: As for "listen not with your mind but with your qi," this can again be problematic. You may be able to get away with saying "listen with your mind" because the mind, after all, is sentient, but qi is not. How can you listen with qi? If the mind listens to qi, what does qi listen to? So how should this be explained? My answer is: when you have become quite accomplished in Jinggong, your mind and your qi will be at one and inseparable. Qi becomes something impossible for the mind to listen to, hence the phrase "You must not listen with your mind." At this point, your mind and your qi, though at one, may not have reached the state of the Void and therefore may still have a slight awareness of your breathing. If you keep on, you will soon lose all awareness of your breathing. During the brief period of transition, rather than listen to qi with your mind and set mind and qi against each other, it makes more sense to listen to qi with qi and wipe out any rift between the two. That's why the instructions say "listen with qi."

Step 4: As for "You should no longer be relying on your ears," and "You should not be relying on your mind, either," a beginner should first try to gather his thoughts together before concentrating on "listening," but carrying this on for too long would be overdoing it. So go on to the next step. Stop listening. By this time, you are moving into the stage of the Void, where your mind and qi are at one, you are no longer aware of your breathing. You may appear to be asleep on the outside, but on the inside, it's another story.

Setp 5: As for "Qi is something unsubstantial. It needs something to form a union with it. Only Dao can merge with the qi of the Great Void. If your mind attains the tranquility of the Great Void, you have made a success of the Mind Tranquility method," after you have gone from the simpler to the more sophisticated stages, you naturally reach the state

Questions and Answers about Jinggong
(Quiet Meditation Exercise)
Therapy for Stress-related Disorders

of the Void without having to direct your mind to it. If you will it, you won't be able to get there. The entire process is to go from what you have acquired to what you were given by nature. So the fifth step should be experienced in the state you were born, but I will not get into that, because it exceeds the limits of therapy. For our purposes, it suffices to reach the state where your mind and your qi merge.

A summary of the three methods cited above: Su Dong-po's method is to begin by counting your breathing, then stop counting and let it be. Zhu Xi's method is to begin by watching your nose, then stop watching it and let everything take its own course. Zhuangzi's method is to begin by listening to your breath, then stop listening and let everything take its own course. The three methods begin differently but end on the same path. Learners can feel free to apply them in combination.

Young patients with stress-related disorders can be 70% or 80% cured by practicing these exercises for three months. Middle-aged patients can be 50% to 60% cured after three months' practice. However, symptoms can vary in degree. I was referring to more severe cases. Those with less severe symptoms can achieve full recovery. After you leave the sanatorium and return to your workplace, it would be advisable to practice twice a day, once in the morning and once at night, and make it a habit. Only then will you be able to keep what you have gained and be fully accomplished in this healing art.

YINSHIZI'S QUIET SITTING THERAPY

By Jiang Weiqiao

Translated by Yang Shuhui and Yang Yunqin

CONTENTS

Introduction

The Quiet Sitting Therapy is a term the ancients used to refer to "internal exercises." In ancient times, the health-conscious engaged in two kinds of exercises—external and internal. Medicine and acupuncture were given to those who were already ill, whereas external and internal exercises were for those not afflicted with illnesses. But these exercises have since become a lost art. Those still engaged in external exercises are ignorant of its techniques. The internal exercises have been appropriated by necromancers, who imposed on them abstract theories about yin and yang, the five elements (metal, wood, water, fire, and earth), and alchemy, thus shrouded them in mysticism that scholars hold in contempt. If something is worth studying seriously, it must contain some truth and therefore should be devoid of any mystic aura. Mysticism appeals only to those who, in addition to having limited knowledge and mental focus, are also averse to serious studies and just blindly follow trends.

Illness dogged my childhood and I had recurrent brushes with death, which is why I started studying this art before I was 20 years old. From 1900 I began to exercise the Quiet Sitting and have kept at it for almost 18 years now. Not only has my long-standing illnesses gone away but I have been feeling more and more energetic. I have long been wishing to use scientific methods to explain the effectiveness of the Quiet Sitting Therapy, but each time I picked up my pen, I put it down almost just as quickly out of a lack of confidence. Far from trying to keep the knowledge selfishly to myself, I have been waiting for the most opportune timing. I recently heard that Okada Konichiro and Fujida of Japan, who advocate the Quiet Sitting Therapy, have tens of thousands of disciples. Okada's followers practice only Okada's version of the Quiet Sitting Therapy. Fujida's books *Breath Harmonization* and *Secrets to Physical and Mental Health* are both the rage and are reprinted dozens of times. After reading them, I was astounded and thought, "But this is a Chinese art! The writings of Okada and Fujida are unpretentious explanations with no claims to mysticism. Their scientific and philosophical approach differs from the teachings of ancient Chinese texts." As I see it, our national inherent character dictates that all knowledge and skills are, more often than not, treated as private property and not to be divulged to the public to benefit. Since time immemorial, goodness knows how many of the very best of our traditions have been lost to posterity. Not so with the Japanese. As soon as they lay their hands on something Chinese that they find valuable, they put their heads together and study it. In the end, they outdo us by far, and we turn around and learn from them. Let me take our external exercises by way of an example. They range from the "eight trigram boxing" on the low end to "fist art" at the top end, but in the tradition of keeping the secrets to oneself, we are reluctant to share the techniques with one another. Hence, those who want to learn them do not get a chance, whereas those who do get to learn them may not learn them well. In the Ming Dynasty (1368 – 1644), Chen Yuanyun traveled to Japan and passed on the art to Fukuno Shichiro, Saemon, and others. The Japanese eagerly took it up and developed it into what is known today as *judo*. In the meantime, our "fist art" remains unchanged. As for the internal exercises, the simpler versions of them could cure illnesses whereas the more refined versions could lead to the attainment of the Dao. However, as they were kept as secrets not to be studied with other people, they end up as something weird and uncanny. Now that the Japanese have acquired them, studied them, and turned them into the Quiet Sitting Therapy, college professors, students, army men, the old, the young, and men and women of that country fall over one another trying to learn it. It has even been incorporated into school curriculums and college students have even formed Quiet Sitting Clubs. How it caught on! Now what about my Chinese compatriots? Still bent on keeping the secrets to themselves rather than passing them on to posterity! How lamentable!

This book is written to dispel all the claims of eerie mysticism and explain the therapy from psychological and physiological perspectives. Everything in the book has been my personal experience. The sections on methods of breathing have been partly borrowed from Okada's writings. Not a word is said on attaining the Dao because, not being sufficiently accomplished in its philosophy myself, I dare not lapse into falsehood.

Our national mood being as inconstant as it is today, many readers are liable to blindly follow what is said in the first book that comes to hand without understanding the reasoning behind it, and interest in a trend hardly lasts beyond the initial stage. Such being the national mood, our country is almost at the brink of collapse. Would this healing art save the day, as the prescriptions of Bianque (China's ancient medical scientist during Warring States Period 475 – 221 BC) had done? Let this book provide the answer.

Yinshizi

Winter 1917

Life and Breathing

A human being must breathe from the moment of birth. Clearly, life and breathing are as inseparable from each other as body and shadow.

The lungs are the chief organ controlling breathing. With each contraction of the lungs, stale air in the body (carbon dioxide) is exhaled through the nostrils. With each expansion of the lungs, air (oxygen) is inhaled through the nose. In physiological terms, this is external breathing. It takes oxygen from the air and delivers it to the blood. At the same time, the carbon dioxide in the blood is released into the air, thus completing an exchange of air in the lungs.

In addition, the blood circulation in the body originates from the heart. Blood from the artery sends the oxygen from the lungs to all corners of the body and allocates it to the tissue of all parts of the body. The carbon dioxide released from the tissue of the various parts of the body is delivered through blood in the veins back to the heart, through the pulmonary artery to the lungs, and then gets exhaled. Oxygen is inhaled and is transmitted through blood of the artery and pulmonary veins back to the heart, and the cycle goes on in what is called blood circulation. The exchange of air between the cells of the tissues in the body is called internal breathing. Therefore, the main function of breathing is to ensure the supply of oxygen in the body and the discharge of excessive carbon dioxide.

The intricate and orderly breathing that takes place inside the body is brought about by the coordination of many organs, a most important part of which is the regulatory role of the higher nerve center and the respiratory center.

As important as breathing is to the sustenance of life and in spite of the abundantly clear explanations now available, many people still believe that only food and drink are basically what sustain life and that the lack of food and drink leads to hunger, thirst, and even death. Little do they realize that breathing is a more pressing need than food and drink. Life can go on for a few days without food and drink, but once breathing stops due to suffocation, death comes in a matter of minutes. This serves as evidence that breathing is even more important than eating and drinking. However, since food and drink must be bought with money, which in turn must be obtained in exchange for labor, and air is to be had for free anytime, one is likely to value food and drink above breathing.

The Sources of Illnesses

Everyone, old or young, male or female, is susceptible to illnesses, which arise from two sources: internal injury and external factors. Internal injury refers to the lack of harmony among the internal organs or damage done to parts of the body. External factors refer to changes in the environment. Both internal injuries and external factors inevitably jeopardize the normal circulation of blood and the exchanges of air in internal and external breathing, thus subjecting the body to illnesses.

Of course, the origins of illnesses are not limited to internal injuries and external factors. Even in these cases, other factors must also be taken into consideration. In short, careful prevention is much better than seeking medical attention after illnesses have already set in.

The Prevention of Illnesses

Chinese breathing exercises handed down from ancient times are quite unique in the promotion of health and the prevention of illnesses. Its subtlety lies in the fact that it is all about breathing.

There are four kinds of exercises: movements of the lower limbs, standing still, sitting, and lying horizontally with relaxed muscles. However, breathing exercises are best done while seated, because when walking or standing, the body and the mind do not easily stay calm, and when lying, the body and the mind are liable to grow drowsy. Calmness comes more easily when quietly sitting, hence the name "Quiet Sitting Therapy." This is a method that has been practiced in China for thousands of years. Its number-one purpose is to regulate blood circulation to prevent illnesses and, if already sick, to heal. Practicing patiently on a daily basis will work wonders.

The Quiet Sitting Therapy

Posture

1. The position of the feet

Illustration 1

Double cross-legged (Illustration 1): This is a method for younger people with greater agility. Rest your left foot and your left calf on your right thigh so that your left sole is level with your right thigh. Then bring up your right foot and place it along with your right calf atop your left thigh, so that both soles face upward and your legs are shaped like a triangle. This is called "double cross-legged." Its advantages are: Since your knees must be pressed against the cushion,

87

your posture will naturally be erect rather than leaning tilted. But this is a posture difficult to learn, and even more so for those of middle age and beyond. So do not attempt this if it is too much for you.

Illustration 2

Single cross-legged (Illustration 2): Place your left foot and calf on your right thigh and then your right foot under your left thigh. This is much easier to do than double cross-legged. Its disadvantages are: Since the left knee cannot be pressed tightly against the cushion, the body is likely to lean toward the left after sitting in this position for some time. But if you start to lean left, you can slowly adjust your position, and no harm will be done.

Crossed-under legs (Illustration 3): For the elderly, if even single cross-legged is unachievable, just cross your legs without attempting to rest your feet

Illustration 3

on your thighs. However, this will not give support to your knees, so the body is even more likely to tilt to one side. Therefore, you need to correct your position from time to time.

Illustration 4

Sitting straight (Illustration 4): If those with leg ailments find the above posture too difficult, they can just sit straight with legs hanging, but be sure to rest the ball of the left foot against the instep of the right foot. Or you can put your feet flatly on the floor but the legs should be at a 90 degree angle to the soles.

Beginners may feel their feet go numb after having sat still for some time. They may slowly relax and assume the posture again after the numbness has gone away. Or they may stand and walk around slowly before sitting down again for another session.

2. The position of the hands

The hands must be totally relaxed. Rest the back of your hand on your left palm, put them gently on your calves near your abdomen. But if you are sitting with your feet on the floor, you may put your hands horizontally on your upper thighs, palms down (Illustration 4).

3. Posture of the head

The positions of the neck, the face, the eyes, and the mouth must all be correct. The neck must be straight, the face forward, the eyes slightly closed, the mouth closed, and the tongue pressed against the upper palate.

4. Recumbent positions

Lying supine (Illustration 5): You can engage in calmness exercises whether walking, standing, sitting, or lying. Of course, it is most difficult to do it while walking and, to a lesser extent, when standing. It takes great accomplishment to do that. Practicing while seated is the most common, so this will be our main focus. Although you can easily grow drowsy while lying on your back, it can be a substitute for the sitting position when it is not convenient or not possible to sit down. You can lie on your back or on your side, as you do when asleep. When

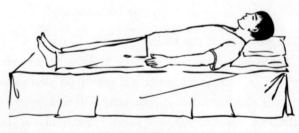

Illustration 5

lying on your back, be sure to put something under your head and shoulders to raise them to a height you feel most comfortable with. See above paragraph for the positions of the eyes, the mouth, and the tongue.

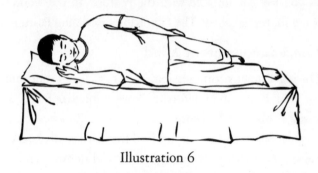

Illustration 6

The Lion King's Reclining Posture (Illustration 6): Although you may lie on your right side or on your left side, it is better to lie on your right side, because you put your heart under pressure if you lie on your left side. When you lie on your right side, keep your eyes, mouth, and tongue in the same positions described above, but lean your head and upper body slightly forward and bend your left leg more than you do your right one until you feel most comfortable with the posture. Rest your left thigh on your right thigh and your left calf and foot naturally behind your right calf and foot. Your right leg should be only slightly bent. Your left arm should be stretched naturally to its full length and your left hand, palm down, should be placed gently on your hip. As for your right hand, turn the palm upward, splay out the fingers, and place it near your head on the pillow for as long as you feel comfortable with the posture. In the world of kung fu, this is called "The Lion King's Reclining Posture."

Concentration of the Mind

During a quiet sitting session, be sure to focus your mind on your lower abdomen (the "lower cinnabar field," located at about 4.33 centimeters, about 1.7 inches, below your bellybutton). Beginners find this hard to do, because various thoughts pass through the mind nonstop and are difficult to harness. Only an accomplished master of the art can disperse such random thoughts and enter a truly tranquil state. How should you go about this? You should begin by guarding against daydreaming when engaged in everyday activities. When it comes time for a quiet sitting session, clear your mind of all thoughts and focus it on your lower abdomen. If distracting thoughts arise again, eliminate them again. Through repeated practice and over time, such thoughts will naturally diminish, leaving the mind completely tranquil and undisturbed. This is the most satisfactory method. If beginners find themselves not up to such rigorous standards, they can close their eyes slowly until only one tiny beam of light is visible, and fix their gaze on the tip of the nose. This is called "Eyelids closing like curtains." Then quietly breathe through the nose until you hear nothing and feel nothing. The mouth must also be naturally closed. If there is excessive saliva, swallow it in small gulps. The most important thing is to be mindful of your "lower cinnabar field." You will find this practice useful.

Another method is to close your eyes slowly and count your breaths. One inhalation and one exhalation count as one breath. Count from one to ten and start all over again, cycle after cycle, all the while focusing your mind. This is called "The body and the mind at one." The positions of the other parts of your body stay as described above. The most important thing remains your attention to your "lower cinnabar field." This is also a very helpful method. Most importantly, it is better to pick one method and stick to it. These methods are all safe and proper, free from side effects. The one method that makes you feel most comfortable in practice sessions will be the one most suitable for you.

Beginners often say, "Before I started learning the Quiet Sitting Therapy, I had few random thoughts. But now, as soon as I begin to get into a quiet sitting session, such thoughts begin to multiply. I wonder why." This is actually a misunderstanding. You see, random thoughts can arise at any time, but they do not normally bother you because your mind is occupied by your engagement with the outside environment. Once you are in a quiet sitting session with your mind focused on your inner body, you will naturally become conscious of the coming and going of complex, jumbled thoughts. This, in fact, marks a preliminary stage of self-awareness. You can take this as a point of departure, do some soul-searching and ask yourself what had led to such distracting thoughts. With practice they will gradually diminish, so do not avoid them.

Beginners may run into two situations: 1. An agitated state of mind that doesn't let you calm down. 2. A state of sluggishness that makes you drowsy. Beginners often start with an agitated state of mind, unable to calm down. And then, with practice, their jumbled thoughts fade away but they get into a drowsy state. This is a common problem for all beginners. There is nothing surprising about this. To pacify the agitated state of mind, you must clear your mind of all thoughts until nothing remains but awareness of your lower abdomen. You will then naturally calm down bit by bit. To overcome the drowsy state, you must try to be alert, fix your gaze on the tip of your nose, and pull yourself together. Generally speaking, at the end of a day's tiring work, you easily get drowsy after you start a quiet sitting session, but if you do it right after you get up in the morning, you will not be bothered by drowsiness because you've just had a full night's sleep.

Breathing Exercises

I have explained above how the process of breathing is the essence of being. It follows that breathing exercises are of crucial importance and merit detailed discussion.

The average person's breathing is often short and shallow. The lungs are not expanded and contracted to their full potential. Therefore, oxygen is not fully inhaled, nor is carbon dioxide fully exhaled, which is why the blood is not clear. And that can lead to illnesses. Following are some pointers for breathing exercises:

1. The exhalations and inhalations must be noiseless. Not even your own ears should hear the breathing.

2. The breaths must be slowly lengthened so that they reach the lower abdomen, but this should be done naturally, without exertion. Practice with patience, and you will be able to succeed.

3. Below the lungs and above the stomach is the diaphragm. Beginners of breathing exercises often feel bloated in the chest. That's because the diaphragm is not being pushed. When inhaling, you must gradually take in fresh air through the nose so as to expand the lungs and push

down the diaphragm. When exhaling stale air, your lower abdomen contracts and pushes the diaphragm up. With the diaphragm going up and down, all pressure in your chest will be released.

4. The large and small intestines are the softest parts of the body. Blood easily gets clogged here. If your breath is deep and long enough to reach the lower abdomen, your abdomen will have the resilience to force the blood deposits out of the abdomen into the limbs.

5. You must breathe through the nose rather than the mouth. Why? Because the nose is meant to be used for breathing. The hair in the nose block dust particles and microbes from entering the respiratory tract. If you breathe through your mouth, you are robbing your nose of its usefulness and, in addition, dust and microbes will enter and cause illnesses. Therefore, you should close your mouth not only during a quiet sitting session, but also in your daily activities.

Its Effectiveness in the Treatment and Prevention of Illnesses

There is no end to the advantages of these breathing exercises for the prevention and treatment of diseases. The exercises work on most chronic diseases that do not respond to medication. Let me cite an example rather than engaging in empty talk: I myself had been plagued in my early youth with a severe case of tuberculosis. There was no cure for it. The Quiet Sitting Therapy was what brought about a complete cure.

At 83 years of age, I can still see and hear well, and I remain agile and free from illnesses. Over the last few years, I have rarely even caught a cold. At sudden changes in the weather or on damp and rainy days, other people may feel out of sorts, but I feel as good as ever. This has been my personal experience with the breathing exercises and what they can do to prevent and cure illnesses.

The Fundamentals

The Beginning of Human Life

Laozi (one of the principal Chinese philosophers and founder of the Daoist school of philosophy of the Spring and Autumn Period (770 – 476 BC), author of the *Dao De Jing—Classic of Morality*) said, "Everything in the universe can be traced back to its roots." In the case of plants, they develop from seeds to buds, from buds to sprouts, and then to stalks and leaves. In their luxuriant foliage, some can reach a height of three meters, some soar into the sky. What makes this happen? It all depends on the depth of their roots. And if the roots can also spread wide, they absorb more nutrition from the soil to nourish the trunks, branches, and leaves. This is common knowledge. As for humanity, which has been in existence for several billions of years, we are just one of the numerous species of this vast universe. Since all life can be traced back to its origin and the origin of plants and trees is known to all, how did humanity begin? Few people have the right answer, although it's actually all too evident. Every creature starts from a cell. The union of a male sperm and a female ovum grows into a fetus, which is the equivalent of a bud. The newborn baby is connected to its afterbirth through the umbilical cord, which falls off after ten months. So we can tell that the navel is where human life begins. Just as plants need nourishment from fertilizers, human beings must be sustained by the mind, and the Quiet Sitting Therapy helps to do that.

The Center of Gravity of the Body

I am not the only one claiming that the origin of human life is the navel. Sages of past had known this all along, which is why they devised the "cinnabar field cultivation method." The "cinnabar field" is located in the lower abdomen, beneath the navel. Since I am writing this to record what I have learned over the years and put everything down in expository form, I have no wish to adopt names like "the cinnabar field," but will say instead "the center of gravity of the body." In physics, an object with its center of gravity in the right place is said to be at equilibrium, whereas an object with its center of gravity in the wrong place will be tilted to one side. Why do tall pagodas and buildings not fall over? Because their centers of gravity are in the right places.

It is deplorable that average mortal beings attempt to reach equilibrium without reflecting on the origin of human life. In their everyday humdrum life, they are so worn down by anxiety and fear of the gods that their minds lose tranquility and their bodies do not follow their will, giving an opening to all manner of illnesses. How pathetic! The Quiet Sitting Therapy, in simple terms, is to focus your mind on the very center of gravity in the body and try to make it reach equilibrium. With practice over time, what you did by effort will become natural. All the cells in the body will follow the will of the mind, dispelling worries and leading to happiness. Tranquility, devotion, and Chan (Zen) advocated by Confucius, Laozi, and the Buddha respectively may differ in moniker, but in essence, what they seek is nothing more than equilibrium of the center of gravity.

The Relationship between the Quiet Sitting Therapy and Physiology

The structure of the human body is so complex and intricate as to boggle the mind. In this day and age, however highly developed science may be, not enough is learned about the human body. In the language of physiology, the first role of all body parts is to sustain life, to absorb nourishment from outside and transmit it to all parts of the body, and to excrete body waste in a process called metabolism. This process never stops during your life span. Its hub is the circulator which includes the heart, the blood vessels, and the lymphatic system. They are what keep the blood circulating nonstop throughout the body. The heart has four chambers and is where blood is pumped out. The blood vessels include the aorta and the veins. The lymphatic system is spread throughout the body, parallel to the veins. It absorbs nutrition and delivers it to the aorta while, at the same time, sends waste to the veins. The blood circulation depends on breathing. With the exhalation of carbon dioxide and the inhalation of oxygen, the blood in the veins goes into the aorta. The entire cycle takes 24 seconds and there are 3,600 cycles and more than 20,000 breaths in a 24-hour period. The fresh air inhaled measures more than 455 square feet. If the blood in a human body is calculated at 2.5 liters on average (Editor's note: nowadays this figure is around 1/13 of the body weight), the blood thus processed comes to more than 7,500 kilograms. Just imagine all these amazing processes going on at such speed without our being aware of them! If breathing is done properly and the blood circulation is unblocked, good health is maintained, but if blockage occurs, the body parts will malfunction. And if injuries are done to them, they, in turn, cause blockage of the blood circulation, resulting in illnesses.

There are various reasons for blockages of blood circulation and the resulting illnesses:

1. Incorrect breathing and improper inhalation of oxygen and exhalation of carbon dioxide.

2. Half of the blood in the body is deposited in the abdomen, so that the abdomen lacks strength, and the stagnation of blood flow causes malfunctions in other body parts.

3. The internal organs are under the control of the sympathetic nerves and therefore do not directly follow instructions from the brain. Even when you are asleep, their functions do not stop, nor do they follow the commands of the mind. So their malfunctions withstand prevention.

4. The beatings of the heart are strongest in the vicinity of the aorta but weaker in the veins that pump blood from the head and the limbs back to the heart. That is why

stagnation is more liable to occur in the veins.

Blood in the human body can be likened to the financial situation in society. Just as stagnation of financial circulation will cause panic in society, stagnation of blood circulation will result in illnesses. But the average person does not take measures of prevention. Health-conscious people do try to promote the circulation by cleaning, exercising, soaking up the sun, and breathing fresh air, but the Quiet Sitting Therapy works best. It fixates the center of gravity in the lower abdomen, as if to strengthen the central government so that it can better direct the various organs of the state. Breathing can be regulated through practice, to push the diaphragm up and down and to make the abdomen strong enough to force out stagnant blood in the abdomen and send it back to the heart. Then the heart will pump out fresh blood and deliver it to all parts of the body. Deeper breathing will make the internal organs more sensitive, so that even if they do not follow the dictates of the mind, they will function better while the heart beats with greater regularity and strength. In such an optimal blood circulation (see the section on Experience for more details), metabolism works perfectly, and illnesses will not occur. Even if you get ill occasionally, you will anticipate it and will soon recover. To prevent illnesses is infinitely better than to treat them after they have already set in.

The Relationship between the Quiet Sitting Therapy and Psychology

What pose more of a challenge to understanding the human being are the mental faculties rather than the body. This involves religion and philosophy. Realists will accuse me of overemphasizing the role of the mind. Believing that everything in the brain vanishes with the demise of the body, they refuse to recognize the role of the mind. At the other extreme, idealists claim that the brain makes everything in the world, and that nothing can exist without the mind. Both are guilty of a lop-sided view. Neither the physical nor the psychological dimensions should be overemphasized at the expense of the other, but there is indeed an abundance of evidence to support the argument that the mind can influence the body. If you feel ashamed, your face will redden. If you constantly worry about something all the time, your hair will turn gray. These are examples of the mind influencing the body. When you are in a happy mood, everything you see or hear or smell is beautiful, but this is not the case when you are feeling low. This is another example of mind over body. When you are in a cheerful mood, you eat with relish, but when you are depressed, you lose your appetite. This is an example of the mind influencing the stomach. Anger, jealousy, or other ugly emotions can poison the blood and the tissue of all parts of the body, which goes to show that the mind also has an effect on the blood. If a hypnotist has someone hold a red-hot stick and says to him, "It's not hot," the man will indeed be impervious to the pain and even experience no physical injury. Examples abound to demonstrate the impact of the mind over the body.

The average person knows nothing of this. With a troubled mind and various temptations assaulting the body, he falls victim to wild, foolish thoughts and loses control over his body. His body then yields to all kinds of addictions that deplete his life force. Illnesses set in, leading to premature death. There is no lack of such examples. Those who practice the Quiet Sitting Therapy can focus their mind and unite with the universe as one. With the body following the dictates of the mind, they enjoy physical and psychological tranquility, stay free from illnesses, and live long lives. What makes this possible? The center of gravity.

The Correct Center of Gravity as Key in the Union of Body and Mind

On a physical level, the center of gravity promotes active blood circulation. Psychologically, it brings scattered thoughts together into focus. Hence, there is actually no distinction between the physical and psychological dimensions. When the center of gravity is in the right place, health improves and the mind enjoys peace. If not, health deteriorates and peace of mind vanishes at the same time. The average person arbitrarily draws a distinction between the two. Those engaged in physical exercises ignore spiritual cultivation, and those engaged in spiritual cultivation dismiss the importance of physical exercises. They all lack insight. The mind is what unites both physical and psychological wellbeing.

The True Meaning of the Word "Still"

The earth revolves around the sun in never-ending motion. We creatures on earth move with the earth. However, if everything in the universe is moving incessantly, where does "stillness" come in? This goes to show that "motion" and "stillness" are not to be understood in their conventional sense. What I mean by "motion" is the movements of the average person against the direction of the rotation of the earth, and what I mean by "stillness" is when the average person does nothing, and just lets himself follow the rotations of the earth. That is why he is not in the least aware of the motions of the earth. Complete stillness—stillness that makes you unaware of the earth's motions—means that you are at one with the rotating earth.

The Correct Location of the Center of Gravity in a Quiet Sitting Session

I have dealt with the placing of the center of gravity in a previous section, and now let me explain what should be done during a quiet sitting session. The center of gravity should be placed in the lower abdomen below the navel. At the beginning of the session, use the breath adjustment method, as explained in the section of Methodology, and apply the entire force of the blood circulation on that spot. A distended, supple abdomen is the external form of a well-placed center of gravity. As for the inside, with the tranquil and worry-free mind concentrated on one point, the inner world is as clean and bright as a moon-lit sky. This is the internal form of a well-placed center of gravity, attainable only by the Quiet Sitting Therapy. Its wonders are beyond description.

The Physical Form and the Spirit

A human being has a physical form and a spiritual side. The average person's attention is entirely taken up with his own physical form and ways to please his ears, eyes, mouth, and body, to the neglect of his spirit. Thus, the center of gravity in his body rises to his chest, and the bad alignment of his body parts leads to illnesses and, worse still, to death from blockage of the qi caused by the misplacement of the center of gravity. Those engaged in cultivation of the body and mind are advised to give equal attention to both. I have noticed situations where athletes with strongly built bodies lose their fight against sudden illnesses and even become disabled. On the other hand, Chan masters or philosophers who cultivate their mind can dispel illnesses and, in spite of their frailness, get to live long lives. Thus, it can be said that the human spirit is far more powerful than the physical form. The Quiet Sitting Therapy lets the center of gravity find safe anchor, so that the spirit and the physical form merge in a union in which the former dominates the latter. Uninterrupted daily exercises can also be called spiritual gymnastics.

Methodology

Now that the fundamentals having been made clear to us let's get down to the specifics. There are two main aspects to the methodology: the right postures and regulation of breathing. These constitute the key to the right methodology.

Posture

1. **Before and after a quiet sitting session, be sure to:**
   (1) Stay in a quiet room. Your current bedroom will

also do. Open the windows, but close the doors so as not to be disturbed.

(2) Have a soft and thickly padded cushion for a sustained quiet sitting session.

(3) Loosen all clothing and belts prior to the session, so that you are not restrained in any way.

(4) Sit straight with your spine erect.

(5) After your quiet sitting session is over, slowly open your eyes and stretch your legs. Do not end the session too abruptly.

2. Position of your feet

(1) Cross your legs, putting the left calf on the right calf, and then the right calf on the left calf (Illustration 1 on page 87). This is called the double cross-legged position, the most ideal of all cross-legged positions. In this position, the knees are pressed against the cushion and the muscles all over the body are as taut as a stretched bow. Sitting straight will prevent you from tilting to one side or the other. But beginners will find this hard to do. The older you get, the greater the challenge. So you do not need to do this if it is too much for you.

(2) Place your left calf on your right calf or vice versa, whichever way you feel more comfortable with (Illustration 2 on page 88). This is called the single cross-legged position. This position is inferior to the double

cross-legged position in the following ways: With the left calf resting on the right calf, there is nothing to support the left knee, so it does not get to be pressed against the cushion, and your body is more likely to lean towards the right. With the right calf resting on the left calf, there is nothing to support the right knee, so it does not get to be pressed against the cushion, and the body is more likely to lean towards the left. Beginners who find the double cross-legged position too difficult can settle for the single cross-legged position, but be sure that you sit straight and do not lean to either side.

(3) The thighs should form a triangle. With the outer side of the thighs pressed against the cushion, the center of gravity naturally stays right beneath the navel. (This refers to the double cross-legged position. In the case of the single cross-legged position, only one thigh is pressed against the cushion.)

(4) Beginners may feel numbness in the legs, but with the passing of time, the discomfort will vanish.

(5) If the numbness becomes unbearable, you may switch the legs. If the numbness persists, you may relax and resume your quiet sitting session after the numbness is gone.

(6) If you can bear the discomfort, it is advisable to let the numbness reach its height. Once it goes over the

peak, it will naturally go away, after which you will never feel numb again in a cross-legged position.

3. Postures of the chest, the buttocks, and the abdomen

(1) The chest. Lean forward a little, so as to lower the pit of the stomach, which means to relax the diaphragm that is located between the stomach and the abdomen. The pit of the stomach is located in the slight depression in the midline just below the sternum. An unstable center of gravity of the body will float up toward the pit of the stomach. A beginner of the quiet sitting exercise will often feel bloated in the chest, which means that the pit of the stomach is too high. Focus on your lower abdomen and relax your diaphragm so that the pit of the stomach feels no pressure. By and by, it will sink lower, letting your center of gravity fall into the right place.

(2) Your buttocks should protrude a little to the rear, so as to keep your spine straight. The spine curves slightly outward at the buttocks, so it is advisable to stick the buttocks out a little when seated, but do not overdo it. Just be natural.

(3) Be sure the center of gravity is securely anchored in the lower abdomen. The center of gravity must be securely anchored in the lower abdomen, but this does not call for physical exertion. Just focus your mind on your lower abdomen, but first, you need to banish all distracting thoughts

from your mind and focus it on the spot about 4.33 centimeters (1.7 inches) below your navel, and the center of gravity will then be securely anchored there.

4. The position of the hands

(1) The hands should be gently held together, placed against the lower abdomen and on the calves.

(2) The thumbs should be crossed and the fingers gently held together.

(3) You may either use your left hand to hold your right hand, or the other way around.

(4) The held hands can rest anywhere, whether on the lower abdomen or on the thighs.

(5) The hands can be left naturally hanging and the fingertips naturally crossed. No exertion of effort is called for.

5. What is to be done with the head, the ears, the eyes, the mouth, and how to breathe during a quiet sitting session

(1) Be sure to face forward and keep your neck straight.

(2) The ears should tune out all sounds.

(3) The eyes should be closed gently.

Some people favor keeping the eyes slightly open, in a posture called "closing the curtains." Closing the curtains is the better option for those who are likely to drop off to sleep while sitting. Those who do not easily get drowsy while sitting is better to keep the eyes closed which helps calm the mind down.

(4) The mouth should be kept closed, and the tongue pressed against the upper palate, so that flesh joins bone.

(5) Breathing should be done through the nose, not the mouth (see later sections for more details).

6. The state of mind during a quiet sitting session

(1) One should forget about everything and refrain from having distracting thoughts.

The human mind is just like a stage and the thoughts are actors who go on and off the stage but are never absent from it. So it is extremely difficult for distracting thoughts not to arise. But if you focus on one thought, other thoughts will subside, so if you focus on the center of gravity in your body, distracting thoughts will gradually disappear.

(2) Use the reflexive method so that distracting thoughts will not arise.

I advised above against having distracting thoughts, but saying so is a distraction by itself. A better option is to use the reflexive method, or, in other words, the inner view method. The average person's eyes see only objects outside the body, never anything inside. Therefore, during a quiet sitting session, you should close your eyes, turn them to your own mind, and sort out the reasons for the rise and fall of distracting thoughts. As soon as one thought arises, use the reflexive method so that it is not reinforced until it vanishes. Do the same thing as soon as a second thought arises. Only by thus tackling the problem at its roots can distracting thoughts stop emerging.

Beginners of the quiet sitting practice often have a misconception. They allege that distracting thoughts increase only after they start the Quiet Sitting Therapy. This is a misunderstanding. The fact is, the average person's mind is filled with distracting thoughts, but those who have never practiced the Quiet Sitting Therapy are not aware of them until after taking it up. This is in fact the first step in self-awareness. Repeated practice of the reflexive method will help gradually reduce distracting thoughts. One must not give up because of the increase of distracting thoughts.

(3) Quiet sitting can eliminate illnesses and promote health, but even the thought of bringing about a cure should also be banished.

(4) Let everything take its own course. Do not seek quick results. It's just like what happens with a small boat that floats midstream. All oars and sails should be put aside to let it just float.

(5) The eyes should be closed during a quiet sitting session, so that they cannot see anything. However, sounds that come through the ears easily arouse distract-

ing thoughts and are the most difficult to deal with. So one should apply the reflexive method to the ears, tune out all sounds, and practice the method long enough so that you would not budge even if a building collapses right in front of you.

(6) Those practicing the Quiet Sitting Therapy must have the faith of a believer in religion. In the initial stage, you may feel low but if you persevere and keep at it, it will work wonders for you. It is faith that makes things happen.

7. The timing of quiet sitting sessions

(1) A truly accomplished practitioner of the Quiet Sitting Therapy can practice it in his mind throughout the day, whether walking, standing, sitting, or lying, but a beginner should set a schedule. It is preferable to practice once every morning right after getting up and every night, before bed. Or at least do one session a day.

(2) The longer a session lasts, the better, but do not deliberately prolong the session. Just let things take their own course. Thirty minutes a day over time will be good enough.

(3) For a busy person, a 40-minute session is recommended, but one hour will be even better.

(4) Mornings or evenings will both do, but for those who can only have one session a day, mornings, after getting up, will be best.

(5) A 15 or 20-minute session every night before bed is quite effective. In short, make sure that you have one session after getting up in the morning. One session at night before bed can be optional.

(6) After waking up, stay in bed and stroke your abdomen and regulate your breath (see more details in later sections). Next, urinate and have your bowel movements, after which you wash your face, rinse your mouth, and then do your quiet sitting sessions.

It is best for quiet sitting sessions to be done after bowel movements. But since everyone's habit is different, those who do not have morning bowel movements can follow their own habits.

Breathing

The breathing process is the essence of being, but the average person only knows that food and drink sustain life and that the deprivation of food and drink means death. Little does he know that breathing is even more important. Food and drink must be acquired with money which, in turn, must be earned through labor. Hence the value of food and drink. As for breathing, since the supply is inexhaustible and is to be had without having to expend labor or money, its value is not fully recognized. However, life can go on for seven days without food, whereas suffocation leads to instant death, which serves as evidence that breathing is more important to life than food and drink. I will be talking about two kinds of breathing: natural breathing and regulated breathing (or reverse breathing).

1. Natural breathing

One exhalation and one inhalation make up one breath. The external breathing organ is the nose and the internal one, the lungs. The pulmonary lobes are located in the lungs, on either side of the heart. When breathing, the lungs expand and contract according to the laws of nature. The average person's breathing mostly does not fully utilize the lungs' capacity and is limited only to the upper part almost without using the lower part at all. Since the exhalation of carbon dioxide and the inhalation of oxygen are not accomplished thoroughly, the blood in the body is not clean and all kinds of diseases arise. This disagrees with the laws of nature governing breathing.

Natural breathing, also called abdominal breathing, must involve the lower abdomen in both exhalations and inhalations. When inhaling, the lungs are filled with air, and the bases of the lungs expand and push down the diaphragm. At this point, the chest is relaxed, and the abdomen protrudes. When exhaling, the abdomen contracts and pushes the diaphragm up until it touches the lungs so that the stale air at the bottom of the lungs is forced out. Although breathing is the function of the lungs, the pulmonary expansions and contractions mostly rely on the movements of the lower abdomen and the diaphragm, in agreement with the great laws of nature, to improve the blood circulation. We must use this method not only in quiet sitting sessions but also when walking, standing, sitting or lying down. Let me list the breath regulation methods as follows:

(1) When exhaling, be sure that the lower abdomen contracts, the diaphragm moves up, and the chest grows tight, so that the stale air at the bottom of the lungs can be forced out.

(2) When inhaling, slowly draw fresh air through the nose and fill the lungs with the air, with the diaphragm going down and the abdomen protruding.

(3) The exhalations and inhalations should gradually grow deeper and longer, so as to reach the lower abdomen and make it firm.

Some people maintain that after inhaled air reaches the lower abdomen, it is preferable to pause for a few seconds in what is called breath suspension. On the basis of my own experience, I advise beginners against attempting this.

(4) The breaths should gradually grow smaller and less perceptible. After repeated exercises over time, you

will lose all awareness of your breathing, as if you are not breathing at all.

(5) When you reach the state described in (4), you are not conscious of the breathing, as if the respiratory mechanisms are useless. It seems that the breathing is by this time done with the pores all over the body. This is the height of the art of breath regulation, but beginners should not deliberately attempt this. It is important to let things take their own course.

2. Reverse breathing

In regulated breathing (also named reverse breathing), the breathing should be deep and soft and long enough to reach the abdomen, just the way with natural breathing. The expansions and contractions are in reverse to what happens with natural breathing, but the purpose remains the same: to make the diaphragm move up and down. Ways to regulate reverse breathing are as follows:

(1) The exhalations should be slow and lengthy, and the lower abdomen should expand and be full and firm.

(2) The lower abdomen should be filled with air, the chest lifted, and the diaphragm relaxed.

(3) The inhalations should be deep and lengthy, the chest should be filled with air and naturally expanded while the lower abdomen should contract.

(4) With the air-filled lungs above and the contracting abdomen below pressed against it, the diaphragm becomes quicker in its movements.

(5) With the chest in expansion, the abdomen may be contracted but it is not empty. Therefore, when exhaling and inhaling, the center gravity remains stable, beneath the navel.

(6) The incoming and outgoing breaths should be gentle and quiet. You should not be able to hear your own breathing during a quiet sitting session.

Some sages maintained that an incoming breath should be longer than an outgoing breath, whereas in our day, some advocate that it should be the other way around. In my experience, the lengths of both incoming and outgoing breaths should be the same.

It can then be concluded that the purpose of both natural breathing and reverse breathing is to exercise the diaphragm. In reverse breathing, unlike natural breathing, you force your abdomen to dilate and contract, so that the diaphragm becomes more flexible and moves more easily. When I first started practicing, I happened to apply the reverse breathing method, which is why I incorporated it in my book. But be advised this method is not for everybody, because it is not as free from potential pitfalls as natural breathing is.

3. Breathing exercises

Natural breathing and reverse breathing exercises share the following similarities:

(1) The cross-legged position as in a quiet sitting session.

(2) The inhalations progress gradually in length.

(3) The breaths should be slow and gentle, quiet and long, and should be gradually directed into the lower abdomen.

(4) Breathing must be done through the nose, not the mouth.

The nose is the right and proper organ for breathing. The hairs in the nostrils are meant to trap dust particles. The mouth is not meant to be an organ for breathing. If the mouth is used for breathing, it will be doing what should rightfully be done by the nose, and therefore cause nasal congestion. Moreover, dust that goes into the mouth easily causes illnesses. So the mouth should always remain closed, not only just during quiet sitting sessions.

(5) With more practice, breathing can be gradually lengthened, until one inhalation and exhalation can take up one whole minute, but do not force anything.

(6) The exercise of quiet and gentle breathing can be done at any time of the day.

(7) Get rid of all worries and thoughts during a quiet

sitting session. If attention is focused on breathing, the heart will not be able to calm down. It is therefore preferable to practice breathing both before and after a quiet sitting session.

(8) Breathing practices before and after a quiet sitting session should be done in a place where the air is fresh. The session should last five to ten minutes.

4. The relationship between the lowering of the pit of the stomach and breathing

I have dealt above with the lowering of the pit of the stomach. It is closely related to breathing. If the pit of the stomach cannot go down, breathing regulation will not be possible and quiet sitting sessions will not be effective. Let me go over that again as it is very important.

(1) Beginners of breathing exercises will feel the pit of their stomach heavy and therefore find it hard to regulate their breathing. This is because the diaphragm is not able to move up and down. You must persevere and not give up.

(2) If you feel your breathing is blocked, do not use force. Let things take their own course and slowly direct your attention to your lower abdomen.

(3) The chest should remain relaxed, so that there is no pressure on the heart during blood circulation. That way, the pit of the stomach will naturally go down.

(4) Over time, your chest will feel lighter, your breathing will become quiet, gentle, deep, and long. The incoming and outgoing breaths will reach the center of gravity beneath the navel, which indicates that the pit of your stomach is lowered.

Abdominal Vibrations during Quiet Sitting Sessions

1. Over time, you will experience vibrations in your lower abdomen, which serve as proof of the firm strength of your abdominal muscles.

2. About ten days before the vibrations occur, you will feel a warm current going back and forth in your lower abdomen.

3. After prolonged to-and-fro movements, the warm current will suddenly burst into vibrations that spread throughout the body. Do not be alarmed if this happens. Just let things take their own course.

4. The speed and duration of the vibrations vary from person to person. This is a natural occurrence. Do not go out of your way to make this happen, nor should you attempt to suppress the vibrations.

5. During the vibrations, let your mind direct the warm current to the sacrum (the lower tip of the spine) and then gradually make it rise along the spine all the way up to the top of your head and then slowly go down the face to the pit of the stomach and, lastly, to the lower

abdomen. (It takes time for you to be able to direct the warm current up the spine and down again to the pit of your stomach. It can happen a few months after the vibrations occur, or even years.) Over time, this warm current can go up and down freely, and the mind can direct it all over the body, to reach even the fingernails and the tip of your hair. Your whole body will feel warm and euphoric.

The reason for the vibrations is quite obscure and difficult to understand. In its circulation, blood is concentrated in the lower abdomen and derives enough strength from there to move around, and the movements generate warmth. But it is beyond my understanding why the warm currents go up the spine to the top of the head and down again to the navel. However, this has been my personal experience and is highly probable. This is what the sages had referred to as "breaking through the three barriers." (The three barriers are: sacrum, the middle portion of the back spine, and the occipital bone.)

The ancients offered multiple explanations for the vibrations, of which let me pick one that makes the most sense. It may not be hard science, but it is not without anything to recommend it. Here it goes: A fetus in the womb breathes not through the nose but through its inner qi that rises up the spine to the top and then down its navel. Once the fetus is born, this channel for breathing becomes blocked and the nose takes over. After long practice of the Quiet Sitting Therapy, one reverts to the way a fetus breathes.

Experience

My Childhood

I was a sickly child, so thin that my parents were afraid I would never live to be an adult. At age 12, I became guilty of masturbation. Over time, I began to experience nocturnal emission, dizziness, backache, ringing in the ear, night sweat, and a host of other ailments. Being young and ignorant, I had no idea what had led to these symptoms. By age 13 or 14, I began to have a slight idea of the cause but remained still very much in the dark. I tried unsuccessfully to get better, but I dared not tell the truth. So I continued to languish in fragile health. Our house was located at the west end of the city, about one mile to the eastern ward of the city. On festive occasions, I would join my brothers in excursions to the eastern ward, but would feel so exhausted that I had to give up midway. After returning home, I would break into cold sweats six or seven times a night. Such was the state of my health in my childhood.

My Youth

After I reached 15 or 16, I was dogged by even more illnesses, including heart palpitations and fevers. I remember that one spring when I was 17 years old, my temperature rose every afternoon and subsided at sunrise the next morning. This went on until the summer when I was 18 years old. Having been sickly for so long, I felt more and more fatigued but I remained a diligent student, often studying late into the night. Being sick was for me the rule rather than the exception, but I was as hardworking as ever in my studies. As a result, my constitution grew even weaker and my ailments more severe.

The Beginning of My Quiet Sitting Practice

When my ailments were at their worst, I tried everything I could think of to seek treatments, but my hometown being in a remote place, only physicians of traditional medicine were available. The doses of medicinal tea they prescribed were so ineffective even after prolonged use that I threw all of them out. Although I did not tell anyone about this, my father figured out the root cause of my ailments and showed me books on cultivation of the mind and told me about the Daoist "Great and Small Circles of the Celestial Sphere" methods for medical use. Only then did light dawn on me, and I took up the Quiet Sitting Therapy. Soon the symptoms went away. However, I lacked perseverance. When my condition got worse, I grew afraid and resumed practice, but when my condition improved, I got lazy and gave up practicing. But at least I realized the importance of taking care of my health rather than ruining it. By age 19, even though the ailments were still with me, I felt healthier than when I was a child.

Continuation of the Quiet Sitting Therapy

After I married at age 22, I believed myself to be healthier than ever before, so I forgot all about the Quiet Sitting Therapy. Failing to restrain my desires, I fell victim to a flare-up of my old ailments. To make matters worse, my irregular eating habits resulted in gastrectasis and esophagitis. I craved food all the time but at meal time, I would lose all appetite. Friends advised me to rest quietly at home, but I dismissed the idea. In the spring of 1899, my brother Yuezhuang died of pulmonary disease. The next year, I also started to cough and soon found blood in my phlegm. Traditional medicinal tea did not do any good. On the contrary, my condition deteriorated. After three months had gone by without any improvement, I was stricken with the fear that I might follow my brother's footsteps. I abandoned all medicine, imposed quarantine upon myself, left my wife and children, and holed up in a quiet room. Thus severing all ties with the world, I devoted myself to practicing the Quiet Sitting Therapy. I was 28 years old at the time.

The Schedule of My Quiet Sitting Sessions

As a beginner, I set up my own schedule. Every morning I rose at three or four o'clock and sat for one or two hours by my bed. At sunrise, I got up, washed, brushed my teeth, ate something, and went out to walk slowly east, toward the sun, to inhale fresh air in an open space. I returned home at seven or eight o'clock. After breakfast, I rested for one or two hours in my room, reading casually books by Laozi, Zhuangzi or Buddhist sutras. At ten o'clock, I would start my second quiet sitting session of the day. After lunch at 12:00 noon, I would walk slowly around my room. At three o'clock, I played my 7-string zither to cheer myself up, or went outside for a walk. At six o'clock in the evening, I returned indoors for another quiet sitting session. I ate supper at seven o'clock. After eight o'clock, I again walked around my room. At nine o'clock, another quiet sitting session. I went to bed after ten o'clock. This was my daily fixed routine with very few interruptions.

The Difficulties for Me as a Beginner

As a beginner, I overdid it out of my anxiety for an early

cure. Distracting thoughts kept cropping up in spite of all I did to get rid of them. Efforts at breath regulation made me feel worse, with the chest as bloated as if it was all clogged up. But since I had faith in the therapy, I kept on practicing, but I grew so exhausted that I almost gave it up. Among the elders of my hometown, there were some who knew well about Quiet Sitting. They said to me when I visited them and told them my story, "You are mistaken. The most important thing in this exercise is to do it the natural way. You should be at one with nature whether walking, standing, sitting, or lying down. Nothing will be gained if you force anything on yourself." These words enlightened me. Henceforth, I stopped doing anything forcibly in my quiet sitting sessions. If I felt uncomfortable, I would rise and slowly walk around the room and resume the session after I felt at ease again. After three months, difficulties vanished and the state of bliss arrived.

The First Vibrations

I started my quiet sitting practice on April 4th, 1900. Initial difficulties did not deter me from persevering in the practice. After I gradually got the hang of it, I became filled with vigor, so much so that I could walk for more than three miles without feeling tired, whereas I used to be able to do only a quarter to half a mile. In every quiet sitting session, I felt a warm current in my lower abdomen moving back and forth. I marveled at this phenomenon. Then, June 25th, my lower abdomen suddenly began to vibrate. Even though I was sitting in my usual posture, my body began to shake almost out of control. To my amazement, the warm current broke through the sacrum and went up my spine all the way up to the top of my head. Six days went by in the same way before the vibrations came to a stop. It had been only 83 days since the April 4th. This was the first time I experience vibrations. Thereafter, in every quiet sitting session, I felt the warm current naturally reach the top of my head along the usual route without shaking my body. All of my ailments—heart palpitations, backache, dizziness, ringing in the ears, spitting blood, and coughing—went away, except my gastrectasis, although the condition did not worsen thereafter.

The Second and Third Times I Experienced Vibrations

During the entire year of 1900, I stayed at home for my quiet sitting practice and politely turned away all visitors. I was determined to subdue the flesh to conserve energy and build up strength, to refrain from talking too much, so as to nourish the qi, and to refrain from straining my eyes, so as to attain mental tranquility. I kept a diary. The initial period from April to June was the most difficult. The effect began to show in June and July. After August, I became accomplished enough to be able to sit for three hours at a stretch. I lost all consciousness of myself and felt spotlessly clean and perfectly at one with the universe.

After 1901, I had no choice but to go out and get a job to make a living. Unable to devote myself to quiet sitting sessions the whole day long, I reduced them to twice a day, one in the morning and one in the evening, a habit that I have kept to this day. On May 5th of 1902, I was in my morning session when the warm current in my lower abdomen began to vibrate again, just as it had done in the June of 1900. The current broke through the sacrum and went up to the back of the top of my head, which is what Daoists call the "jade pillow." The vibrations lasted for three days until my back parietal bone ached, but I was not surprised. Suddenly I felt as if my parietal bone had cracked open and the warm current kept going around the top of my head. This recurred at my subsequent quiet sitting sessions but the vibrations did not happen again. So this was the second time I experienced vibrations.

On the November 15th, the abdominal vibrations came back. The warm current went around the top of the head before going down my face to my chest and back to my lower abdomen. At this point, the vibrations stopped.

This was the third time. Thereafter, the warm current would ascend to the top via the spine and go down my face to my lower abdomen in recurrent cycles. When I caught a cold and felt ill, I would summon the warm current with my mind and make it go around my whole body, to reach even the fingertips and the hairs. After some time, I would break into a sweat, and the cold would be cured. From that time on, my old ailments never bothered me again, and I was able to climb mountains with my friends and walk for several miles without feeling tired. What is most interesting is my 28 miles trek from Jiangyin to Wujin in 1902 when I learned in Nanjing Shuyuan (an academy of classical learning) of Jiangyin. I got into a contest with a friend in the summer vacation, and started the trip from Jiangyin in the morning and reached Wujin at four o'clock in the afternoon. I did not feel at all tired, walking under the blazing sun.

My Research on the Subject for More Than 20 Years

I began to study the quiet sitting art when I was 17. I was driven to it by my ill health, not by any deep faith in it. I found the Daoist writings on yin and yang, the five elements and alchemy so elusive and difficult to understand that I practiced it only off and on without taking it seriously. I didn't make it a daily habit until age 28 when I was diagnosed with pulmonary disease. However, being a proactive person by nature, I took quiet sitting sessions merely as a way to conserve energy, as something to help me stave off illnesses. I did not quite believe what the sages said about cultivating "the cinnabar field" and clearing the three barriers. It was only after I personally experienced vibrations on three occasions that I came to see the truth of what they said. Only then did I realize that there were too many truths in the world for me to understand, and that the sages' words should not be dismissed out of hand.

What the sages said about inner exercises are in fact ingenious ways to build up health, but their origin is no longer known. After the Qin (221 – 206 BC) and Han (206 BC – 220 AD) Dynasties, alchemists began to concoct elixirs of longevity, their principle being identical to Laozi's tranquility and the Buddha's meditation. Regrettably, their methods have been lost to posterity. As a result, the average person looks down on them as black magic. The virtuous deem it beneath their dignity to even talk about them, and the ignorant know nothing about them. How pitiful! With these apprehensions in my mind, I have long been wishing to write this to make them known to the public.

Since 1903 I came to Shanghai till the publication

of this book at the age of 42, I have been doing two quiet sitting sessions a day—once in the morning and once at night—without interruptions. For more than ten years, apart from flare-ups of hemorrhoids or other ailments needing surgical attention, I have not been ill year in and year out. In my recent readings of books on philosophy, psychology and medicine, I have come upon much writing about the Quiet Sitting Therapy I practice. I learned that the fundamental principle of the Quiet Sitting Therapy is in making the human mind dictate the body to promote blood circulation. (See the section on the Fundamentals for more details.) As a part of my practice, I always walk east in the direction of the sun. Whereas I had done this before in compliance with instructions in Daoist books, to absorb the vitality of the east and the essence of the sun, I now learned that this is, in fact, in line with the medical theory advocating greater exposure to sunlight and fresh air. Moreover, since sunlight kills bacteria, such exposure is most beneficial to patients of pulmonary diseases. I had been taking daily walks outdoors in order to stretch my legs that had grown numb after quiet sitting sessions, but now I learned that these walks are in line with the medical theory advocating more physical exercise. But what is the secret that lies behind the

Quiet Sitting Therapy?

Chen Tuan (? – 989, a scholar recluse of Five Dynasties about whom legends abound), in his hermitage on Mount Hua, had slept for more than a 100 days. Bodhidharma had spent nine years in meditation, facing a wall. These are historical facts. Meditation is popular with previous generations, especially among the elderly. According to Daoist records, the first step to immortality is the art of quiet sitting. Since it has helped cure my ailments, I suppose that, by extension, eternal life may be possible. However, being a person prone to hands-on experiences, I dare not make statements not borne out by my personal experience. Everything I say is factual.

Be Sure to Forget Everything in Quiet Sitting Sessions

When I first started out, I packed my schedule too tightly in my eagerness for quick results. I add this information about my personal experience for your benefit. It is preferable to practice twice a day, once in the morning and once at night. You need not do it too frequently, as I did, to avoid problems. I cannot overemphasize the importance of not forcing anything, and the best way to avoid forcing anything on yourself is to forget everything. If the purpose of your quiet sitting practice is to cure an illness, you must banish the thought of seeking a cure when you are in an actual quiet sitting session. If you aim to promote your health, you must also banish the thought of promoting your health when you are in a quiet sitting session. Your mind must be a total blank. The Quiet Sitting Therapy takes effect by bringing about gradual changes to your body and mind. If you are constantly hoping for a cure or for better health, your mind will not know tranquility and therefore the effect will be compromised. This was what happened to me when I first started out. So I feel compelled to caution you against it.

Do Not Seek Quick Results

Many of my friends who know about my quiet sitting practice come to me and ask for instructions, but only a very few out of hundreds succeed. Most of them fail because they are too eager for quick results. They witnessed my success without realizing that I succeeded precisely because I do not expect quick results and I do not give up. There are no tricks to it. They start with a brave beginning but then, seeing no improvement, they give up. Some even suspect that I have secrets that I hold back from them. Little do they know that the Quiet Sitting Therapy is a method of cultivation of the body and mind, which is not unlike the nourishment that comes from food. If you seek quick results from food nutrition and overeat, you do damage to your stomach. Would you then give up eating? Have you ever heard of such a ridiculous thing? The right approach is like taking a long-distance journey. You take your time making the journey and eventually you reach your destination.

Vibrations Have Nothing to Do with Effect

I have said before that after prolonged practice of the quiet sitting exercise, there will be vibrations in the body, but whether this happens or not or how frequently this happens depends on the constitution of the person involved. Some people think the therapy does not work because they experience no vibrations and therefore they give up practicing. Some worry about the absence of vibrations in their bodies as they witness it happening to other people. They are all mistaken. People vary in their constitution. Some people experience vibrations several months after they start the practice. Some experience vibrations several years after they start out. Some have no vibrations at all, even though they have already experienced changes in body and mind. Thus it appears that there is no co-relationship between vibrations and effect.

The Relationship between Quiet Sitting Sessions and Sleep

Doctors advise eight hours of sleep every night for the average person. For a married couple, sharing the same bed is not the best option, because the carbon dioxide they exhale poisons the air, and the sick one will contaminate the healthy spouse. This applies to Quiet Sitting Therapy devotees as well. It is preferable to start a quiet sitting session at nine o'clock in the evening, go to bed at ten, and rise at six in the morning for another session, and more importantly, one should sleep alone. After I first started out in 1900, I slept alone for one whole year and achieved the fastest results. I have not been able to abstain from sex for the last few decades but I still like sleeping alone and have been doing so all along.

The Relationship between Quiet Sitting Sessions and Food

Doctors advise moderate food intake at fixed hours and slow mastication. These are all words of wisdom. We Chinese like overeating. There is an ancient poem that includes the line, "Try an extra helping of rice!" When we inquire after each other's health, we ask, "How many bowls of rice can you eat?" We assume that a large appetite means you are full of vigor, but in fact, overeating burdens the stomach, and indigestion leads to illness. Parents always urge their children to eat fast, without knowing that if you don't chew your food well, your stomach and intestines will have to overwork, thus resulting in illness, and your teeth are more likely to decay if they are under-used. If you do not eat your meals at fixed hours and if you eat too much cookies and other snacks, you cause nonstop secretion of your gastric juice. These are all causes of stomach ailments. From childhood on, I loved eating fast and not at fixed hours, which was why I ended up with gastrectasis. After I started quiet sitting sessions, I gradually came to see how wrong I had been. Nowadays, my meals are only one third of what they used to be. For breakfast, I have nothing but one bottle of milk. I used to get hungry often even though I ate a lot, but now, with reduced food intake, I do not easily get hungry but, instead, feel more vigorous than before. It can thus be seen that the feeling of hunger does not arise from real hunger but is actually an abnormal feeling that one experiences because one's stomach is accustomed to fullness. Eating less enables you to chew more slowly, which is good for digestion. This is an irrefutable truth.

The Combination of Motion and Stillness Exercises

Since ancient times, there have been external and internal exercises to build up health. External exercises are exercises of motion, like the Eight-Section Qigong Exercises (Ba Duan Jin) and taiji that have gained popularity recently. If you devote yourself to quiet breathing exercises only, to the neglect of exercises of the body, you put yourself at the risk of health disturbances. Therefore, breathing exercises must be combined with motion exercises. Eight-Section Qigong Exercises is the simplest. Taiji is more complicated and needs an instructor. If you have no time to learn, you can just settle for daily calisthenics exercises. Internal exercises include many varieties but all of them are based on breathing exercises and quiet sitting practices.

In my previous writings on quiet sitting practices, I never brought up external exercises. That was a mistake. I have been practicing taiji for more than twenty years, but only recently have I realized its huge benefit to breathing exercises and quiet sitting practices. So motion and stillness exercises should not be done to the exclusion of each other. External exercises alone without internal exercises will not do, and vice versa, a point that I cannot overemphasize to you.

Conclusion

This little volume is written in language as simple and easy as I can, with no scholarly theories. You should have no difficulty understanding it.

This method of health building has been practiced in China for thousands of years by people who did it alone and passed it on to only a few disciples. Because they kept it a secret to themselves and refused to share it with the public, it has sadly not enjoyed wide circulation. However, in recent years, the Quiet Sitting Therapy has caught on in various parts of the country, and statistics show that a substantial number of people practicing it have cured chronic diseases. This is exciting news!

With this, I conclude this volume on my experience in breathing exercises and quiet sitting practices over the last few decades. I have more students than I can count.

ACKNOWLEDGEMENT

I would like to express my gratitude to all those who gave me the help and support to complete this book. I especially want to thank Mr. Liu Xun of Rutgers University who specializes in the social and cultural history of Daoism in late imperial and modern China. Professor Liu provided me with professional and valuable suggestions with regard to the book's framework and its titles, and offered other ideas related to the introduction. Also, I want to thank him for introducing me to Dr. Wu Yakui, an expert on Quanzhen Daoism of the late imperial and early Republican era. Mr. Wu recommended for translation a small tract written by the celebrated Daoist Chen Yingning and entitled "Questions and Answers about Jinggong (Quiet Meditation Exercise) Therapy for Stress-related Disorders." I hereby thank them both for their kind and professional assistance which has helped bring this book to our readers.

—*The Editor*

This book is edited and designed by the Editorial Committee of *Cultural China* series

Managing Directors: Wang Youbu, Xu Naiqing
Editorial Director: Wu Ying
Editors: Yang Xinci, Zhang Yicong, Susan Luu Xiang

Introduction by Yanling Johnson
Questions and Answers about Jinggong (Quiet Meditation Exercise) Therapy for Stress-related Disorders by Chen Yingning and translated by Yang Shuhui and Yang Yunqin
Yinshizi's Quiet Sitting Therapy by Jiang Weiqiao and translated by Yang Shuhui and Yang Yunqin

Interior and Cover Design: Wang Wei
Cover Image: Quanjing

ISBN: 978-1-60220-128-6

Address any comments about *Quiet Sitting: The Daoist Approach for a Healthy Mind and Body* to:

Better Link Press
99 Park Ave
New York, NY 10016
USA
or
Shanghai Press and Publishing Development Company
F 7 Donghu Road, Shanghai, China (200031)
Email: comments_betterlinkpress@hotmail.com

Printed in China by Shenzhen Donnelley Printing Co., Ltd.

3 5 7 9 10 8 6 4 2

The material in this book is provided for informational and entertainment purposes only and is not intended as medical advice. The information contained in this book should not be used to diagnose or treat any illness, disorder, disease or health problem. Always consult your physician or health care provider before beginning any treatment of any illness, disorder or injury. Use of this book, advice, and information contained in this book is at the sole choice and risk of the reader.

The China Written Works Copyright Society (hereof CWWCS) has been commissioned to transfer the author remuneration of portion of the written works used in this work. Relative copyright holder shall contact CWWCS.

Contact CWWCS:
Telephone Number: 010-65978906
Address: 4F, Commercial Building, Jing Guang Center, Chaoyang District, Beijing, China 100020
E-mail: Chinacopyright@yahoo.cn